6

m

*

3 9077 01000908 5

WWC

W9-CKH-785

j 025.218 B422s   WWC

Beilke, Patricia F.

Selecting materials for and
 about Hispanic and East
 Asian children

Rochester Public Library
115 South Avenue
Dept. of Work with Children

Rochester Public Library

page edges stained 1-24-94

SELECTING MATERIALS
FOR AND ABOUT
**HISPANIC AND
EAST ASIAN
CHILDREN AND
YOUNG PEOPLE**

SELECTING MATERIALS
FOR AND ABOUT
HISPANIC AND
EAST ASIAN
CHILDREN AND
YOUNG PEOPLE

P A T R I C I A F. B E I L K E

AND

F R A N K J. S C I A R A

Library Professional Publications
1986

© Patricia F. Beilke and Frank J. Sciara
All rights reserved
First published in 1986 as a Library
Professional Publication, an imprint of
The Shoe String Press, Inc.
Hamden, Connecticut 06514

Printed in the United States of America

Library of Congress Cataloging-in-Publication Data

Beilke, Patricia F.
  Selecting materials for and about Hispanic and
East Asian children and young people.

    Bibliography: p.
    Includes index.
    1. Libraries and foreign population. 2. Libraries,
Children's — Book selection.   3. Libraries, Young people's
— Book selection.   4. School libraries — Book selection.
5. Spanish Americans — Books and reading.   6. Asian
Americans — Books and reading.   7. Bibliography — Best
books — Children's literature.   8. Bibliography — Best
books — Young adult literature.   9. Bibliography — Best
books — Spanish Americans.   10. Bibliography — Best books
— Asian Americans.   I. Sciara, Frank J.   II. Title.

Z711.8.B44   1986   025.2'18089   85-23920
ISBN 0-208-01993-6

CONTENTS

PART 2: INTRODUCTION

PART 3: INTRODUCTION

PREFACE

As the Hispanic American and East Asian American populations rapidly increase in the United States today, the youth of these cultural backgrounds require many more books and other materials from which to learn about themselves. At the same time, other American youth must learn more about these age cohorts with whom they will share a lifetime in our multicultural society. However, one difficulty with this is that most librarians and teachers who work with children and young adults in this country have ethnic backgrounds that are not of Hispanic or East Asian origin, so in order to do the job of selecting and using materials in this area they must grow both in attitude and knowledge in ways that will facilitate their development of programming and learning opportunities.

This book begins an exploration of some of the professional growth possibilities that may be undertaken by library media staff members: (1) inservice education and development, (2) additional reading about various cultural groups; (3) development of increased awareness of ways to identify biases and stereotypes in materials; (4) adapting or reexamining guidelines for selection of materials; (5) seeking guidelines which indicate the effects of materials on young users; and (6) developing new ways to provide supportive services for the families of the children and young adults who immigrate to the United States. These professional learning activities can result simultaneously in providing opportunities for children and families whose forebears came in the previous migrations to the United States to increase their appreciation of the cultures of their new neighbors. Even though this book focuses on backgrounds of people from several selected countries, many of the ideas and concepts have applications for other ethnic or minority groups and can be adapted with little effort.

ACKNOWLEDGMENTS

Conversation with the editor, Virginia H. Mathews, led to the development of the topics of this book. Her interest and guidance have been appreciated.

Many persons have contributed information from which the authors have learned, especially individuals who shared their knowledge and their publications who work with agencies listed in *Fair Textbooks: A Resource Guide*, United States Commission on Civil Rights Clearinghouse Publication 61 (Washington, D.C.: U.S. Government Printing Office, 1979).

Special appreciation goes to the librarians who provide materials and services for the following institutions: Anderson College, Anderson, Indiana; Ball State University, Muncie, Indiana; College of Librarianship, Aberystwyth, Wales; Information Center on Children's Cultures, United Nations Children's Fund (UNICEF), New York; McGill University, Montreal; the New York Public Library; United Nations School; University of Texas, Austin; and the Yonkers Public Library and the Queens Borough Public Library, both in Jamaica, New York. In addition, sincere appreciation is expressed to personnel who provided information to the authors at the Asia Society, New York, Midwest Bilingual Education Multifunctional Resource Center, Arlington Heights, Illinois; Center for Mexican-American Studies, University of Texas, Austin; Institute on Pluralism and Group Identity, New York; Proyecto LEER, The

Texas Woman's University, School of Library Science, Denton; and the University of Texas, Asian Studies, Austin.

The contributions made by twenty-eight public and school librarians in response to the nationwide study described in chapter 5 are gratefully acknowledged.

Suggestions made by library colleagues, including members of the Ethnic Materials Information Exchange Round Table, have been helpful. Appreciation is expressed to Pat Bromley, David Cohen, Jean Coleman, Melinda Greenblatt, Sharad Karkhanis, Anne Pellowski, Adriana Acauan Tandler, Lucille C. Thomas, Ana Torres, Patrick Valentine, Phyllis Van Orden, Mitsuyo Woodward, and Marie Zielinska.

Special contributions have been made by colleagues and friends who read and provided suggestions: Edward W. Barth, Ruth Jane Barth, F. M. Hemphill, Juanima Wells McLaughlin, and Vladimir F. Wertsman.

The support provided by the authors' respective colleges, the College of Applied Sciences and Technology and the College of Education, Ball State University has contributed to the publication. The interest and encouragement of Dr. Roy Weaver, Associate Dean, College of Education, has been appreciated.

Essential to the publication have been the assistance of Sherry Hartmann in organizing materials and survey responses, the bibliographical assistance of Mary Wolcott, the preliminary typing of Garnell Jones and Rhonda Peek, and the final typing by Sally Minnick.

The book is divided into three parts of two chapters each. Part 1 addresses the context in which public and school library services are presently provided and discusses possibilities for inservice activities related to serving immigrant or minority populations in other countries. Part 2 provides brief background descriptions, with recommended readings, for learning more about several cultural groups of Hispanic Americans and East Asian Americans. Part 3 examines information about the evaluation of materials related to minority and immigrant groups: (1) provided through text materials commonly available for instruction concerning literature for children; and (2) reported from a nationwide inquiry about selection guidelines and inservice procedures related to the selection of materials for and about Hispanic Americans and East Asian American children and young people. In addition, Part 3 describes several types of guidelines for the selection and use of materials and several types of assistance available through some of the federally and privately funded resource centers.

Reassessment of information needs and the quest for better ways to meet these needs are ongoing endeavors. Development of personal networks of alternative possibilities can enrich the lives of information-providers as well as information-users.

PART 1
INTRODUCTION

Children and young adults are nurtured formally and informally through their association with others: persons who live with them in families and neighborhoods, and persons who serve their learning and informational needs in schools and libraries. The environments in which children dwell influence their present and future growth. Institutions supported by the general populace to serve the young have enormous potential for influencing the attitudes and the actions of children and young adults, now and long after they have left their youth behind them.

The number and kind of books available to children and young adults is known to influence their lives. Greater quantities of books and other reading materials are to be found in the homes of children and young adults who demonstrate effective reading skills and develop lifelong habits of reading and learning. Self-identity and self-image developed by individuals when they are young is a deep concern of both educators and librarians. So also is the perception and subsequent treatment of others by children and young adults. These things are greatly affected by the content of materials, and are therefore a matter of concern to all who nurture children and young adults: their families, members of their communities, educators, and librarians. Content reflects truly the dignity and worth of people of all cultures with accuracy and that affirms the diversity which exists in our society can promote positive growth.

The contents of materials reflect the prevailing attitudes and philosophies of the time at which the materials are developed. Persons who study the history of literature for children find that historical and sociological conditions influence not only what is included in the materials but also which of the materials produced are selected as useful and appropriate for children and young people.

Chapter 1 indicates some of the current conditions in the context of which materials are selected for children and young people. Persons who are responsible for the selection of materials find that their selections are always made under constraints imposed by the social and economic environment of the times. The shortage of funds to purchase resources is a perpetual problem for those who serve children and young people in schools and public libraries. In public libraries, budget requests for children's and young adults' materials must frequently compete with the budget requests for materials intended for adults.

Chapter 2 indicates some approaches advocated for inservice or staff development for persons responsible for selecting materials to meet youth's informational needs related to many cultures. This chapter draws upon the experiences also of those who provide library services in other countries. As social conditions rapidly change, those concerned with the selection of materials must reassess, replace, and add to their store of knowledge, as well as their attitudes. Selection guidelines must be revised to reflect changes in the populations served, and in beliefs about the nature of society and how it evolves.

Chapter 1
Selection of Materials in the Context of Library Services

COMMUNITY NEEDS

Selection of library materials in school and public libraries is made in terms of the library services which are provided in a given community. Library services take place within a socio-political environment. One of the strengths of library services in the United States is the importance placed on meeting particular informational needs based upon knowledge of the community served. Awareness of community characteristics has been long advocated as important for all individuals who provide library services, who must understand with special sensitivity the attitudes held by individuals within the community.

Just as community needs and attitudes should govern the ways in which services are offered by libraries, so they should be reflected by the appropriateness of materials to be added to library collections. Sensitivity to community attitudes includes learning about those that vary within ethnic groups and by generations. First-, second-, and third-generation attitudes may vary greatly. Sylva N. Manoogian describes the diversity of ethnic communities as including the native born as well as new immigrants, monolingual as well as multilingual persons.[1] Manoogian indicates that user needs reflected in requests may be associated with education of self, and may include meeting language and survival needs, in addition to historical, cultural, and literary interests.[2] Manoogian says that library staff members need assistance in developing awareness concerning the needs and attitudes within ethnic communities as well as with individuals who may not be familiar with cultures other than their own.

The Funding of Library Services

Much of the funding for both public library and public school systems is provided by a combination of state and local public tax funds, a small but essential proportion of which come from the national level. There are also some funds, mostly for special purposes and projects, supplied by the private sector.

The present status of state and national support of library services is geographically uneven and fraught with political and economic uncertainties. As this book goes into production, the administration has completely "zeroed out" of the budget all federal funds for libraries. In the case of school library media programs, it had loaded the block grant to the states, within which these programs must compete for funds, with an increased number of competitive eligible programs. This situation exists against a backdrop of exponentially increasing illiteracy, and of the inability of millions to obtain entry-level jobs because of inadequate education and of older persons to retrain themselves for jobs in new industries. It occurs at a time when a U.S. Department of Education's National Commission on Excellence in Education has found the nation to be at risk and in need of the very kinds of educational reform which libraries alone can make possible.[3] It has followed directly the publication by the U.S. Department of Education of *Alliance for Excellence: Librarians Respond to A Nation at Risk*,[4] in which, in his foreword, the U.S. secretary of education asserts that "To assure survival in this difficult age, there is need to elevate the United States to the standard of a lifelong Learning Society. Schooling must be more demanding because so much more is being demanded of us—as adults, parents, employees, citizens, voters and consumers. Somehow, families must hear this message. Somehow they must be led to accept the urgency of creating a Learning Society and, to that end, supporting with energy the tough recommendations of *A Nation at Risk.*.

"The challenge before us is of such magnitude, though, that school and family will be a match for it only when they forge a grand alliance with a third institution—the library."

The needs are hardly new, but the need to satisfy them has become increasingly acute as the 1970s gave way to the 1980s. Yet library support, without which they cannot be met, is threatened at every level.

The first White House Conference on Library and Information Services, held at the end of 1979, produced some priorities for action which speak quite directly to the concerns that are the topic of this book. Those priorities, ranked six through ten,[5] addressed the need for: development of a system to improve the sharing of resources; enactment of a national library act that includes categorical funding; the mandate, under federal direction, for establishment of adequate library media centers staffed with certified personnel for all elementary, middle and secondary schools; public relations; and that "all learners, regardless of age in residence institutions (including correctional and medical), race, disability, or ethnic or cultural background, should have continuing access to the information and materials necessary to cope with the increasing complexity of our changing social, economic, and technological environment."

Finally, as part of the current evidence from the grass roots that books and other library services and materials must remain, and be accorded budget increases on, federal, state and local fiscal agendas, there is the resolution by the National Council of Teachers of English on "Increasing Funds for Books," passed by the membership at the November 1984 annual conference of NCTE:[6]

> that the National Council of Teachers of English reaffirm its belief that ease of access to books is essential to achieve excellence in education; that NCTE affirm its support for the standards established by the American Library Association for School Libraries [sic]; that NCTE endorse the recommendation of the Secretary of Education that schools increase threefold their expenditures for library books, texts, and other instructional media; and that NCTE urge governors, chief state school officers, state legislators and, where appropriate, local government agencies to commit resources to increase the number of books and other reading materials and make them accessible to all learners, especially preschool children in low socioeconomic areas.

Remarks from a speech by Major R. Owens, then a New York State senator and now a member of Congress, characterize the environment in which library services are offered at present in the United States. Owens reflected on the polarized concerns within the library community:[7]

> On the one hand, there is an enthusiastic focus on the infinite possibilities for service improvements through technological gains, including electronic communications, computerized data bases, coin-operated information bands and other similar devices.
>
> At the other extreme, there is a preoccupation with devastating budget cuts, the emasculation of school libraries, the astronomical rise in prices for books and other materials, and other similar survival problems in libraries.

The need for coordinated research and demonstration programs concerning library services to underserved users and to potential users persists today as surely as it did in 1975, when Childers discussed the right of access to information by all persons.[8]

Meeting Needs of Cultural Minorities

In 1983, the report of the Task Force on Library and Information Services to Cultural Minorities was published by the National Commission on Libraries and Information Science (NCLIS).[9] NCLIS had convened this task force in 1980, to report to it by the close of 1982. The task force chose to limit its study and recommendations to the four major cultural minority groups in the U.S. — Afro-Americans, American Indians, Asian Americans, and Hispanic Americans (all of them primarily nonwhite) comprising altogether about one-fifth of the nation's population. Recommendations for improvement in assessing the informational needs of these populations and in meeting them numbered forty-two, grouped under Library and Information Needs, Library Personnel, Services and Programs, Materials and Resources, and Funding.

Several broad and general concepts regarding libraries and a multicultural society governed the work of the task force:

- that the concept of a multilingual and multicultural society is desirable and should be affirmed;
- that libraries are essential to all segments of society, providing basic information to support education and the democratic process, and preserving the record of our heritage and culture;
- that responsibility for library service is a tripartite obligation of local, state, and federal levels of government;

- that libraries play an important and unique role in the integration of cultural differences within the community;
- that public libraries as community institutions have a unique role in the dissemination of information to all persons in society without fees; and
- that all libraries can assist cultural minorities, the fastest-growing segments of the population, to become equal participants in society through access to information.

Among its findings, the NCLIS Task Force pointed out that "minorities are growing at a faster rate than the population as a whole, and during the next three decades, the proportion of the American population of white and of European ancestry will decline at a rapid rate." These demographics, said the task force, have "serious implications for America's economic planning, the educational system, and library and information services. . . . Since minorities will constitute a major segment of the work force and will contribute substantially to the economic well-being of the nation, the United States government must be certain that its minority populations receive quality education and are guaranteed access to library resources and information."

In other findings, the task force found that "fiscal constraints have limited the outreach and other programs that have been beneficial to minority communities. . . . Programs considered significant to the service of cultural minority groups include community information and referral services, oral history projects, library cable television programs, ethnic history and cultural awareness projects, consumer protection education projects, multimedia ethnic materials, and computer-assisted instruction. These programs must be developed in concert with minority communities."

The task force found, in the area of funding, that funds for services for minorities have come primarily from federal dollars, and that because of severe cutbacks in these funds many programs addressed to cultural minority needs have been eliminated by library administrators. The recommendation is that libraries stop relying on external funding for such programs and services, and make support of them a part of the library's regular budget. The task force came out strongly against publicly supported libraries charging fees that "create barriers to the use of library and information resources and services by minorities."

Included with the NCLIS Task Force report is a special study, performed with NCLIS support, in connection with the task force's work.

This is a Needs Assessment Study of Library Information Service for Asian American Community Members in the United States,[10] undertaken by the Asian-Pacific American Librarians Association (APALA). Says the report, ". . . the picture that these statistics present—almost total neglect of the information needs of Asian Americans in terms of budget, collection, programs and staff on the part of nearly half of the libraries participating in this survey—is more than enough to turn all potential Asian American library users away from the libraries' doors."

Needs assessments and training for Asian American professional library personnel were the focus of other recommendations in the cultural minorities task force report that have been supported strongly in other quarters. David Cohen, director of the Institute on Ethnicity and Librarianship at the Queens College Graduate School of Library and Information Studies, City University of New York, pointed out, however, the importance of all library personnel being involved in meeting informational needs with ethnic materials and programs. In testimony connected with the first White House Conference on Libraries, in 1979, Cohen concluded with a quote from page 2 of the Guide for Developing Ethnic Library Services, developed by the California Ethnic Services Task Force:

> The ultimate goal of every public library should be complete integration of services to the point where a separate ethnic component is not necessary. Ideally, ethnic and ethnic-oriented staff should exist at all levels in the library, from top administration to pages. Inclusion of ethnic needs in the planning of programs and services should be constant and automatic. All library staff should be interacting with the community, not just designated outreach librarians.[11]

Success Factors in the Education of Minorities

The significance of the growing diversity of youth in schools and communities is a major concern of the president of the Carnegie Foundation for the Advancement of Teaching and former U.S. Commissioner of Education, Ernest L. Boyer.[12] Thirty percent of the high school students in the United States are members of minority groups. More than half of the twenty largest school districts have a majority enrollments of minority youth, many of whom, says Boyer, have not been well served by public education. The challenge goes beyond that presented to the schools, to the people of the United States.

To assist each child to reach the potential that exists at birth, Boyer suggests that schools focus on formal learning in the early years and place top priority on language; strengthen counseling; flex academic scheduling to accommodate those who need to work; and, most important, influence parents to increase their involvement with the education of their children.

A. Harry Passow reports that recent positive signs concerning urban education have been observed.[13] Francis Chase, who directed the Urban Education Studies project between 1977 and 1980, identified ten factors found in various forms in sixteen urban school systems which had contributed to the revitalization of education:

1. collaborative relationships between schools and community organizations;
2. involvement of parents and other citizens in all phases of educational planning and instruction;
3. establishment of alternative schools;
4. added provision for early childhood educational programs;
5. emphasis on instruction in basic skills;
6. the initiation of bilingual and multicultural programs;
7. new programs for the handicapped;
8. expansion of roles for creative and performing arts;
9. establishment of systems for instructional management;
10. development of system-wide planning, management, and evaluation.

Three significant trends were cited as being observed in all sixteen of these city systems: (1) participation by minority groups and the poor in educational decisions; (2) attention to advice from groups and persons outside the education profession; and (3) collaboration between schools and community organizations.[14]

Passow concludes that the way in which educational planners and decision-makers in the 1980s relate their activities to the larger urban problems of housing, employment, recreation, and health will determine the shape of urban education in the future.[15] It is in these same urban areas that Thomas C. Battle claims public library services are frequently unavailable.[16]

Some Library Models and Guidelines

An exemplary effort to serve community needs in an urban area is that of the New Americans Project of the Queens Borough Public Library,[17] which "serves residents of Queens whose primary language is other than English. The Project works closely with ethnic community organizations and branch libraries to assess local needs, link residents with existing neighborhood and system-wide library services, and create new services." Special services and programs of the New Americans Project include: (1) "Mail-A-Book"—foreign language books-by-mail service available to readers of Chinese, Greek, Italian, Korean, Russian and Spanish. In those languages the potential readers receive descriptive lists distributed by branch libraries and community organizations; (2) "English as a Second Language"—free courses in English available at the Central Library and branch libraries in communities with many limited-English-speaking residents; (3) "Materials"—records and cassettes for learning English, and popular books and magazines in foreign languages distributed system-wide; (4) "Foreign Language Films"—free feature films, with English subtitles, shown at branch libraries; (5) "Programs and Performances"—celebrations of art and literature of community ethnic groups, that utilize artists who live in the community. Music, dance, drama, and bilingual poetry readings are among the types of programs offered. The need for coping-skills programs is assessed by the project staff with assistance from community agencies. Appropriate programs are offered in selected branch libraries.

In 1984, The New Americans Project staff, Adriana Acauan Tandler, Alan Wagner, and Elizabeth Hsu, produced a manual entitled "Library Services to Non-English-Speaking Populations, The Queens Model: A Directory of Service Agencies."[18] Inquiries about the manual can be directed to Adriana Acauan Tandler, Community Specialist, or Alan Wagner, Assistant Community Specialist, Queens Borough Public Library, 89–11 Merrick Boulevard, Jamaica, New York 11432. This directory is intended as a model for other library systems which plan to gather and compile information to provide improved library services to their limited English and non-English-speaking populations. The directory is a result of a Library Services and Construction Act, Title I Bilingual Invitational Grant, awarded to the Queens Borough Public Library in 1983 by the State Library of New York.

Microcomputers were used in the design, compilation, and editing of the directory. The directory lists 164 representative agency entries and shows only a portion of the information collected. The directory includes lists of book dealers and distributors, a description of the process used to make contacts with community organizations, and copies of questionnaires used to gather initial and follow-up information. A section entitled "Some Aids for Library Service to New Americans" is especially useful for librarians and teachers. Included are recommended listings of books, periodicals, vendors, health materials, guidelines for library services, and bibliographies.

Many of the informational and educational activities of the New Americans Project exemplify trends identified by Passow as those which characterized successful educational programs in school systems. Public libraries provide many educational programs. It is evident that key factors of working closely with individuals and agencies within the communities they served characterize successful educational activities offered by both public library and public school systems.

Patricia Tarin and Yolanda Cuesta provide extensive and useful guidelines for the provision of library service to Spanish-speaking Americans.[19] These guidelines can be adapted by persons who wish to provide library service to persons who speak languages other than Spanish. The guidelines have been reviewed at a REFORMA (National Association of Spanish-Speaking Librarians) Program. The importance of involving the Spanish-speaking population in needs-assessment, planning, implementation, and evaluation is stressed in the guidelines.

Development of the collection should be based on formal and informal evaluation of community needs, including those of potential as well as present users. These guidelines advocate that selection criteria and procedures be established for the evaluation of library materials which are acquired or replaced. These guidelines recommend that selection policies include specific provisions for serving the Spanish-speaking population.

Materials upon which information services are based must include: survival information, knowledge of the community, and new databases or directories for currently unmet needs. Guidance is given about the need for cultural sensitivity so that nationality, language, and dialect preferences will be considered. Inclusion of materials not typically collected in libraries is encouraged, e.g., *fotonovelas* (novels in picture form) and children's literature in the form of comic books, which are popular in Latin America. Literature should be acquired that presents positive models of persons of Latin heritage for children and adults.

Uses of General Terms

Sensitivity to community needs and attitudes begins with an accurate appraisal of the terminology preferred in a given locality. Preferred terminology varies by communities and within communities. Connotations associated with certain terms in a given locality may be more important than dictionary definitions. Terms used in the present publication may not, in some instances, be those preferred by a given group in a specific community. Indeed, common understandings are not easily agreed upon among members of some cultural groups.

Some terms are more appropriately used in specific contexts. The use of generic terms should be avoided when more specific designations can be used, and examples of those which should be replaced by more specific terms when applicable are given in the Pennsylvania Department of Education's *Guidelines for Creating Positive Sexual and Racial Images in Educational Materials* (adapted from *Guidelines*, developed by Macmillan Publishing Co., Inc.).[20] The generic terms of "Hispanic Americans" or "Spanish-speaking Americans" should be avoided when the more specific designations of "Mexican American" or "Cuban American," related to the country of origin, can be used. Similarly, "Asian American" should be replaced by country of origin designations, such as "Chinese American," "Japanese American," and "Korean American" whenever possible.

For purposes of this publication, an important term to consider is that of "culture." Many books and articles discuss the term "culture." One of the helpful discussions is that provided by Donald T. Mizokawa and James K. Morishima.[21] They explain the concept of each human being sharing similarities and differences with other human beings. Mizokawa and Morishima identified a useful definition of "culture" as that submitted by Kroeber and Kluckhohn in 1952 after a review had been made of 150 definitions:

> Culture consists of patterns, explicit and implicit, of and for behavior acquired and transmitted by symbols, constituting the distinctive achievement of human groups, including their embodiments

in artifacts; the essential core of culture consists of traditional (i.e., historically derived and selected) ideas and especially their attached values; culture systems may, on the one hand, be considered as products of action, on the other as conditioning elements of further action.

Another term for which a common understanding is needed is that of an "ethnic group." An "ethnic group" is defined by James A. Banks as "a group which has a unique ancestry, the members of which share a sense of peoplehood, and which has some distinguishing value orientations, behavioral patterns, and political and economic interests."[22] Banks says that members of a given ethnic group are likely to view the world from a perspective that differs from the perspectives of members of other ethnic groups. For instance, Anglo-Americans, Irish-Americans, and Italian-Americans are members of different ethnic groups. He says an "ethnic group" should not be confused with a "racial group." Banks says that an ethnic minority group is frequently politically and economically powerless within a society. Examples of ethnic minority groups identified by Banks are Black Americans, Jewish-Americans, and Chinese Americans.

"Race" is a term which changed as scientific information about blood types led to new designations, sometimes called geographical races. According to Pamela L. Tiedt and Iris M. Tiedt, the three former designations of European (white), African (black) and Asian (yellow) have been replaced by nine groups: African (Negroid), American Indian (Amerindian or American Mongoloid), Asian (Mongoloid), Australian (Australian aborigine or Australoid), European (Caucasoid), Indian, Melanesian (Melanesian-Papuan), Micronesian, and Polynesian.[23] The Tiedts refer their readers to up-to-date encyclopedias for additional discussion of the topic.

Some terms are heavily freighted with political and legislative connotations. One example is the term "bilingual." "Bilingual," in addition to its dictionary definition, evokes strong and diverse responses among various individuals and groups because of the concept of "bilingual education."

The development of bilingual education in the United States is discussed by Tiedt and Tiedt from the period following World War I, when the emphasis in public schools was on English only, to the present, when the initial emphasis on language has expanded to include bicultural as well as bilingual attention. "Some forty-six languages have been represented in bilingual educational programs supported by national funds. Tiedt and Tiedt present a brief but frank discussion of bilingual education: the English-as-a-second-language approach, whereby emphasis is on instruction in English; the full support of the primary language, at least throughout elementary school, in a dual-language approach to instruction, which requires teachers competent in both languages and children in the class whose primary language is English to use also the other language in which instruction is provided; and the opposition of some parents to any bilingual approach. Bilingual instruction may be opposed as a hindrance to the development of competencies in English or because of stigmas that may be associated with special programs of instruction.

Tiedt and Tiedt suggest some goals that can be as useful for public and school librarians who plan multicultural programs as they are for teachers: that students appreciate the diversity within society; identify groups within the United States and describe their contribution; note similarities of needs and behaviors among people; identify differences among individuals; synthesize understandings gained from study and discussion of relevant literature; and evaluate experiences gained from their studies.

School and public librarians can, as Tiedt and Tiedt advocate for teachers, serve children and young people through:

1. display of appropriate behavior in talking with other persons as individuals, not as stereotyped representatives of a sex, race, class, or ethnic group;
2. promotion of open discussion of practices or language which hurt others or limit opportunities for their development;
3. planning of programs which can lead to less stereotyped thinking; and
4. selection of materials which are not stereotyped.

Changes have occurred in society and, thus, changes have to evolve in library services and programs. Yukihisa Suzuki observes that the evolution proceeds from an old approach—orientation toward interests of the majority—to a new approach that reflects the needs and desires of ethnic minorities.[24]

Among the ways in which librarians and teachers can make positive contributions to their respective communities is through the use of appropriate behaviors in working with others as individuals, the planning of programs whereby cultural as well as linguistic information can be shared, and the selection of materials to meet cultural as well as technological needs.

Both in the provision of resources within schools and libraries and in the development of instructional and informational programs, the trends indicative of excellence and relevance show that increased participation in materials-selection processes and program-planning processes by the youth and their parents as well as the general public should be encouraged.

Chapter 2
Inservice Training /
Staff Development

The Challenge in an International Context

Our problems of inadequate library services to multicultural populations in the United States are not unlike those prevalent in other countries. Commenting on this, two Australian authors preface their article with the following: "The major task confronting all Australians is not to decide whether Australia is a multicultural society. We have a multicultural society. The first challenge is to make it work."[1]

The same concept can be applied here at home. Some organizations and individuals are loath to recognize the multicultural composition of our country, even fostering a "we" and "them" attitude. The myth of the "melting-pot" theory still prevails in some minds, with the notion that sufficient legal and social pressure will cause members of various immigrant groups to the United States to deny their own cultural, racial, and ethnic identities and backgrounds and acquire white, middle-class perceptions, values, attitudes, and habits.

There is much evidence to support the notion that too-rapid acculturation of immigrant groups creates marginal people — people with mixed perceptions of self-identity who hold membership in their ethnic group as well as membership in the at-large society, yet do not really "fit" into either goup. From Australia comes this insight about immigrants (known as migrants in Australia):

> We believe that hostility and bitterness between groups are often the result of cultural repression. We were informed, and

observed ourselves, that some parents and their children had drifted apart because of what is referred to as the cultural gap. In these cases, the children at school or work observed that the way of life of their parents was quite foreign to their associates and was sometimes the object of ridicule. Rather than be seen as someone odd or different the children had rejected their parents' culture and attempted to take on another identity. They lost their native language and much of their culture in this process and became alienated from their parents. We observed that the trauma occasioned by the cultural gap has other effects. It is damaging psychologically and is an impediment to education, thus preventing individuals from achieving their full potential.[2]

Additional evidence of the need for strengthening cultural identity for immigrant groups comes from Sweden, from those who work with "visiting workers," many of whom became permanent residents. The "visiting workers" represent approximately 12 percent of the total population, come from widely differing cultures, and speak about 130 different languages.[3]

In the past, the chief goal of immigrant services had been rendering assistance to immigrants in adapting to life in Sweden. This goal remains, but with some additional concerns because of new findings resulting from psychological studies on immigrants:

Research on the psychological effects of emigration and immigration has shown that relatively pleasant and successful integration into the new society is best achieved if immigrants have a strong personal linguistic and cultural identity. It is believed now that, although social integration should be the goal of all aid extended to immigrants, full cultural integration is not desirable, because only a strong cultural identity of origin and language will lead to successful adaptation.[4]

Cultural institutions in Sweden, such as public libraries and schools, actively support the home cultures and languages of the immigrants. By law, children whose home languages are other than Swedish must attend two hours of instruction in school per week in their languages. Libraries must provide support materials for the multilingual and multicultural population. Such materials include reading materials, as well as "other cultural materials and services (records, tapes, films, exhibitions, prints, etc.) that are normally supplied by public libraries."[5]

A special project, which has a history dating back to pre–World War I, provides library services to immigrant children. This is the International Youth Library (IYL). As the only special library for children's literature in the world, the IYL has been involved in the promotion of new awareness of minority literature for teachers, librarians, and children. These efforts go beyond the provision of literature for immigrant children. Walter Scherf states, "It is not enough to bring books in original language to children of immigrant and minority groups; children native to the host countries too must be introduced to the cultural and social problems of the newcomers. This introduction can be done partly through translated works."[6]

Movement from one country to another has been typical of human beings since time immemorial. Problems and opportunities in the United States in regard to immigrants are similar to those in other countries, but on a much larger scale. Library services can play a much more important role in the acculturation process than many people seem to be aware. Although it may be difficult for those who work in library services with immigrant clientele to understand fully the deep emotional trauma caused by uprooting, this kind of understanding is necessary if real motivation to serve effectively is to occur. Commitment could come about naturally from interaction with immigrants, but this does not appear to be likely to happen frequently, as many of the immigrants bring no associations with library services from their homeland. A powerful message which details many of the problems experienced by immigrants as they attempt to cope with their new environment (country) is one by S. Simsova, herself an immigrant and a librarian.[7]

Writing about the adjustment process of immigrants, Simsova states, "A marginal man is not marginal until he experiences the conflict of the two cultures as his personal problem. This is a shock to him and for a time he suffers from a double consciousness. He becomes estranged from both cultures and frequently also from the transition group (the company of other marginal men)."

Psychological reaction to marginality is individual and manifests itself in a variety of behaviors, from discomfort or slight insecurity to extreme stress and trauma. Somehow the immigrant must find his / her place in terms of degree of acceptance or rejection from the majority group.

It should be noted that Simsova states that members of the second generation who may suffer a different but just as severe sense of marginality as their parents, usually prefer to read in the language of the new country. They can avoid many of the problems of second-generation marginality if they do not turn against their parents' original culture and are enabled to explore it. In this endeavor she feels the public library can play an important role.

As Australia looked at its responsibility for library services to new immigrants, mainly those from countries in southern Europe, South America, and the Middle East, and refugees from Southeast Asia, there came the realization that immigrants from these countries "lack a strong tradition of public library service."[8] Because these immigrants are not naturally attracted to library services, must not libraries reach out to them? Responses to this question included the following:

1. Public libraries were not serving those unable to read English, and had not taken cognizance of the changing nature of Australian society and the concomitant need for public librarians to change their attitudes on the provision of library service.
2. The extent to which people made use of public libraries depended on level of education, e.g. the higher the educational level attained, the greater the use of public libraries. There was also a correlation between level of education and socioeconomic status.
3. Those people from countries with a strong tradition of public libraries made greater use of library services than those from countries lacking an effective library system.

The United States, with large numbers of immigrants from Hispanic and Asian backgrounds, can use findings such as these to redirect library efforts for immigrant populations. It is estimated that the number of legal immigrants to the United States in 1984 will be more than double the number of twenty years ago. This dramatic increase from 292,248 in 1964 to 610,000 in 1984[9] signals frantically for a new direction of effort for library service in the United States.

Evidence seems to indicate that a joint and common effort by a variety of social agencies, including libraries, is mandated to assist immigrants in identifying with and maintaining their original cultures and identities while beginning the slow and often painful journey towards acculturation in their new homeland. Clearly, libraries have a central function to perform.

Preparing for Inservice Training

Reports of staff development which encourage library personnel to serve more effectively the needs of Hispanic American and Asian-Pacific American clientele have been sparse. A common response, even in the largest cities, is to employ personnel with Hispanic or Asian backgrounds and utilize them, mainly, for book selection. While such an approach is better than totally ignoring the needs of these groups, it has definite limitations. Investment of such responsibility in a single person, or a few people, seriously restricts the base on which a library service operates. Through a *planned* staff-development approach, the entire staff can be motivated and assisted in seeking solutions to the recognized and unrecognized needs of Hispanic and Asian groups.

The overall objective of staff development is the improvement of professional behavior. A carefully planned program not only presents new knowledge but attempts to influence attitudes, as well as improve skills. Effective staff development programs avoid the "top-down" pattern, in which the chief administrator is "in charge" of all phases. This is not to say that top-level administrators can avoid proposing suitable topics or establishing goals and timetables for staff development. It means that once these have been identified, provision is made for wide involvement of various levels of personnel, and that there is a certain amount of latitude within which staff can organize and work to achieve stated goals.

With these very limited suggestions for an effective staff development plan, attention will be focused on the tasks to be accomplished and on some suggested approaches toward their accomplishment. One of the initial problems is the failure to recognize that there is a problem of delivery of adequate library services to Hispanics or Asians. As Rubin states:

> Professionals do not often conceive of themselves as culture bound. The objective attitudes and scientific procedures which form the foundation for their training and functioning stress freedom from personal bias and adherence to formal codes. The essence of their expertise is said to be in their ability to judge a situation solely on the basis of factual and analytical criteria. Indeed, what separates them from other people and endows them

with status and authority is precisely their superior capacity for rationally approaching and solving problems.[10]

Coupled with Rubin's concern is another consideration relating to the philosophical premise that undergirds any library operation. The authors have taken the position that the personnel of any library service, whether of a public or school nature, are not reactive only but must be pro-active as well in terms of the learning that takes place in the community. Acceptance of this premise translates into tangible and observable activities on the part of library personnel. Libraries are far more than storehouses of knowledge and information; they are also presenters of information and learning opportunities which reflect community needs and offer solutions to community problems. Library personnel *relate* to the community's people.

The inservice program advocated by the authors should assist participants in learning to:

1. identify and locate ethnic groups within the service area of the library;
2. become familiar with the culture of specific ethnic groups, as well as their past and present problems;
3. obtain materials appropriate for users' needs;
4. identify the kinds of library programs most needed by the ethnic groups identified (this step especially involves members of each group);
5. plan and carry out library service programs for the ethnic groups identified; and
6. evaluate the effectiveness of such programs.

Adaptation of these elements should be made to "fit" a particular situation.

Identifying and Locating Ethnic Groups

Just as the pluralistic nature of American culture is often ignored on a national level, so this is often true also at the community level. The social majority — usually white, often of Anglo-Saxon origin — may be thought of as representing the community, while minorities, particularly if they are Hispanic or Asian, are not given the level of recognition due them — or the services. While some communities have remained fairly stable in their ethnic composition, others undergo change which, for quite a long while, can be overlooked. One of the first steps in developing any inservice program for library staff is to help librarians and teachers to learn to perform an ethnic analysis of the community, town, county, or school district. With the rate of change being what it is, this assessment should be done every five to ten years, depending on the locality and its size.

Many of the approaches advocated for becoming ethnically aware can be particularized for specific application. Useful suggestions can be gathered from the *Ethnic Studies Handbook for School Librarians* (ED 167 460), prepared by Frances Haley and others,[11] and *Teaching Ethnic Awareness*, by Edith W. King.[12]

While some staff members become motivated to make changes in their procedures and programs because they have been made aware that the number of Hispanics or Asians is increasing in the community they serve, many will not. Maintaining the status quo rather than changing is natural to most humans, and recognizing this, a staff inservice approach in the affective domain would seem to be in order. How to help people change their ingrained emotional responses and attitudes is a question not easily answered. However, some approaches have been tried with a reasonable degree of success.

One strategy involves having each staff member explore the effects of ethnic membership on his or her own early years of socialization. How did each one become a unique person? If ethnicity may be defined as "a sense of peoplehood, a sense of commonality derived from kinship patterns that include a shared historical past, common experiences, religious affiliation, a common linguistic heritage, as well as shared values, attitudes, perceptions, mores, and folkways,"[13] then there are many dimensions of ethnic membership.

Those with high ethnic identity should be encouraged to share the sense of the protective mantle that ethnic membership bestows, to give one a strong sense of belonging. Those born into families with strong ethnic identification will probably have telling personal experiences to relate.

Others may have low ethnic identity themselves but be able to bring experience of ethnic influences to the group from having lived in or near a neighborhood or community with an identifiable ethnic membership.

The highly sensitive and personal nature of this activity requires that the discussion leader carefully establish the proper mood within the group, so that honest and sincere revelation of experiences and insights are allowed expression in an atmosphere of freedom and receptivity. If the proper climate for the experience cannot be effected, because of the diverse attitudinal range of the group or for other reasons that could cause the activity to become a negative experience, then it should be avoided.

As individuals share the results of interaction with one or more ethnic groups, both the positive and negative aspects should be identified. Positive aspects may include cultural contributions such as foods, specific linguistic expressions, colorful holidays, art, music, etc. Negative aspects cited may include being misunderstood, being victims of prejudice and discrimination, lack of trust, or exclusion from the life of the mainstream society. Ethnic membership, especially ethnic minority membership, is a double-bladed sword. On one side, ethnic membership in America can give one identity and a strong sense of belonging. On the other side, minority ethnic membership can mean denial of opportunity, so that true equality is always a dream, never a reality.

From this beginning, then, the question can next be addressed of which ethnic groups are represented in the community served by the library. An ethnic profile can be constructed on a school building or community neighborhood basis. Many schools will collect information regarding the ethnic composition of individual schools, but often this information is gathered in such broad categories, as Hispanics, Asians, etc., that further refinement is necessary. Census tables which detail social characteristics by state and by county are often available. But again, while census tables can identify broad groups, some further refinement and specific identification of ethnic groups is necessary.

Social services organizations or social clubs of various ethnic groups are often listed by the local chamber of commerce. In some communities, ethnic heritage studies may have been funded in the recent past, so that in-depth studies of Hispanic or Asian groups may be available. Several of these projects resulted in a directory of ethnic groups within a city and a listing of the various social organizations, with titles, addresses, and contact persons specific to a certain ethnic group. Many of the listed organizations offer the availability of demonstrations or talks to outside groups in order to increase ethnic understanding and appreciation.

The use of the telephone directory can be of assistance in identifying various ethnic groups.[14] "Let your fingers do the walking," and in the white section, *note surnames*, since Hispanic or Asian surnames can often be noted. If the telephone book is large, then divide the book into sections so that several persons can work on this task at the same time. The yellow pages can also be searched, noting Hispanic or Asian surnames of physicians and dentists. Ethnic restaurants can be identified as well.

While some persons can be readily identified by surnames and easily associated with the correct country of origin, others, of course, cannot. Churches or other places of worship are good sources of information about the size and whereabouts of a given ethnic community, and clergy will probably be very helpful contact persons.

After learning how to gather, or actually gathering, information with which to identify, quantify, and locate Hispanic and / or Asian group populations in the library's service area, small group sessions can help workshop participants to sort out and categorize facts and steps to action. Discussion in small groups provides opportunity for sharing a wide variety of insights, observations, and opinions about the situation. From the initial steps of recognizing the existence and numbers of Hispanic and / or Asian group members, there will need to be an intensive effort to find out what the problems and needs of the people in these groups really are. Interaction among members of the small groups is beneficial because it allows an individual not only to share attitudes and ideas with the group but to be influenced by the ideas expressed by others as well. This kind of process holds the potential for helping each person to accept, reaffirm, reject, or revise ideas concerning these minority groups.

A list of facts about the presence of Hispanic and Asian populations can be developed from the discussions of the small workshop sessions. These are givens, such as "Our library service area has 9,500 Mexican-Americans in it." The list would detail in what areas of the community they live, with breakdowns by age, occupation, and level of educational attainment. A second list which could be developed at this point is one of *general* actions to be taken, as "The library should increase its collection of materials which relate to Mexican-Americans." It is a pretty safe bet that this action will be necessary no matter what direction the services take. As the staff development sessions proceed, participants will return to these two lists of basic facts and actions to be taken, revising and fine-tuning them as more information becomes available.

Introducing unfamiliar library services to groups unfamiliar to the library staff is more complex than it may sound at first. People who may be unused to the concept of an open society which offers information freely and openly to everyone may find it difficult to overcome their wariness. There must be a great deal of admittedly time-consuming give-and-take between the library staff and members of the target communities. Asking people what materials and services they would like when they do not know what is possible or available does not work well. There must be some materials visible at the start, and some indication on the part of the library staff of what kinds of services they might be able to offer if desired. It is a process of give-and-take, trial and error, aimed at building the expectations of the new-user communities as they grow in confidence to choose and to express their choices of materials and services.

Learning about Culture

Culture is defined in various ways. Some teachers, or those in teaching roles, include as cultural activities such things as the use of travel posters or piñatas, cooking and eating tortillas or rice dishes, or constructing origami figures during art period as methods of understanding another culture. Some may also include songs or folk dancing of a particular country as an effective means of experiencing another culture.[15] Culture so defined is too narrowly defined, however, according to King, who identifies this as a common pitfall.[16]

A broader definition would seem to be appropriate if a deeper and more encompassing understanding is to be engendered: "Culture includes all of the rules for appropriate behavior which are learned by people as a result of being members of the same group or community, and also the values and beliefs which underlie overt behaviors and are themselves shared products of group membership."[17]

Knowing something of the culture of an ethnic group is necessary if some level of true understanding, acceptance, and appreciation is to develop among inservice participants. Although it is interesting and enlightening to learn about the home country and the traditional and historical culture of the potential client group, the main focus should be on their present-day "transition" culture as they try to adapt themselves to life in the United States.

An important consideration, as we have said earlier, is that ethnic groups within larger general categories, such as Asians, be studied not as Asians but as Japanese, Chinese, Koreans, and others. There will be some common characteristics found in these various cultural groupings that are categorized in broad geographic terms, but generalizations are to be avoided.

Another consideration in studying an ethnic group is to "critically analyze all information for the effects of stereotyping, recognize the facts of acculturation, and be sensitive to individual differences."[18] It must be remembered that acculturation is a dynamic process in which individuals of the same ethnic background will "travel" at various speeds, arriving often at different "destinations."

Finally, it should be remembered that the critical test of learning about the culture of a particular ethnic group, Mexican-Americans, for example, is knowledge of and understanding about what is happening to those members of the group who are living right in the library service area under study. Reading accurate materials and listening to well-informed speakers generalize about the target group may be helpful in providing background information, but the bottom line is to understand the situation of those the library is gearing up to serve. This means sorting through the generalizations to find those that fit the real people to be helped.

Areas to be included in the study of an ethnic group's culture will have to be carefully selected, and choices will have to be made too about the varying depth of coverage required from area to area. It seems that there is never enough time allocated for inservice activities, too often because a "one-shot" approach is tried. In fact, inservice development should take place over time, because it takes *time*, and a number of sequenced group and individual activities, to change attitudes, increase knowledge, or improve skills.

Banks[20] gives some areas in which to examine and compare ethnic groups, which could well be used as an outline for study:

1. Origins—determine if the group is native or immigrant, and if immigrant, determine the reasons for moving.
2. Discrimination—judge if the group is experiencing discrimination and the kinds of discrimination. If no discrimination exists, determine why.
3. Culture—identify the cultural and ethnic groups' unique characteristics.

4. Assimilation—determine the degree of cultural and structural assimilation.
5. Economic status—assess the economic status and decide if there are problems.
6. Education—appraise the degree of difficulty young people are experiencing in obtaining an education and determine the reasons for success or failure.
7. Power—determine the degree of political organization as well as the political power of this group.
8. Ethnic revitalization—Estimate the degree of ethnic revitalization in this group.[19]

These concepts would seem to concentrate heavily on the sociopolitical aspects of a cultural group. While this is very important, it is far from the whole story. Many other aspects of a culture which could aid inservice participants in understanding need to be considered. Additional areas which could be added can be drawn from a very usable listing provided by Saville-Troike in a chapter titled "Questions to Ask about Culture."[20]

Although aimed primarily for teachers in bilingual-bicultural programs, the areas as stated are comprehensive and could be utilized as guidelines for inservice study. Areas selected from this listing would depend upon the present knowledge of the inservice group, as well as the time frame allowed for such activities. Each area is explained well in Saville-Troike's book, with several questions stated for each concern.

Cultural areas to be explored include the following:

1. General—avoid stereotyping and blanket applications to *all* members of the ethnic group.
2. Family—consider family composition, authority, children's roles, interrelationships, and structure.
3. Life cycle—assess the importance and significance of the varying life stages from infancy to old age.
4. Roles—judge the available roles, method of acquisition, and expectations.
5. Interpersonal relationships—study acceptable method of greeting, male / female interaction, how difference is expressed and resolved.
6. Communication—consider the varieties of oral and written languages used, characteristics of well-spoken language, sex roles

related to language, and use and meaning of nonverbal communication, as gestures or body postures.

7. Decorum and discipline — assess commonly accepted means of
social control and discipline through authority and role expectations with consideration given to age and sex.

8. Religion — understand commonly recognized religious roles,
authority, and manifestation of religious practices such as dietary
restrictions, fasting, death, etc.

9. Health and hygiene — determine commonly accepted standards
of body hygiene as well as acceptance of modern medical practices, the use of folk medicine, and beliefs, taboos, and practices.

10. Food — consider types of food eaten, frequency, social rules regarding food, medicinal uses of food, and any taboos or practices
associated with food.

11. Dress and personal appearance — study types of dress to determine clothing which is typical, as well as that worn for special occasions. Consider restrictions imposed for modesty, the symbolic
significance of color, relationship of dress to group identity, and
the dress differences for age, sex, and social class.

12. History and traditions — learn about persons or events important
in their history, method of perpetuating their history, festive celebrations related to their history, the extent to which this group in
the United States identifies with the history and traditions of the
home country, and the circumstances of immigration to the
United States.

13. Holidays and celebrations — understand the purpose and importance of holidays and celebrations in terms of cultural values in-
culcated or group socialization.

14. Education — determine the purpose of education as perceived by
the group, preferred methods of educating and learning, differing expectations according to sex, accepted student behavior,
and responses in a learning situation, and expected years of
schooling for children.

15. Work and play — consider the range of behaviors regarded as
work and those regarded as play, with kinds of work considered
prestigious, the value of work, and the purpose of play.

16. Time and space — investigate the cultural concept of time as it
relates to punctuality, speed, the seasons, or order. Space can be
considered in terms of how individuals organize for meetings,

in children's encounters, and taboos or preferences for different directions.

17. Natural phenomena—determine the extent to which the group accepts either traditional or scientific theory regarding natural phenomena, such as rain, thunder, lightning.

18. Pets and other animals—assess attitudes and beliefs toward animals as pets, for religious significance, behavioral prescriptions, or taboos.

19. Art and music—learn about forms of music and art considered of most value, media and instruments used, and any taboos.

20. Expectations and aspirations—determine the expressed future goals for children and adults, and the propriety of an individual expressing future goals. Determine the degree of desire of parents to have their children learn English and assimilate into the dominant culture.[21]

After the areas of cultural inquiry have been determined, the learning mode to be used in an inservice workshop setting should be established. A single mode has been shown not to be the most effective. Many methods of learning are possible, but which are available? Four approaches are presented for consideration: (1) presenters from the ethnic group being studied; (2) presenters from other community agencies that serve the ethnic group being studied; (3) independent study by workshop participants utilizing a range of print and nonprint media; and (4) field study completed by workshop participants. A combination and variety of learning modes should be seriously considered if the resources can be made available.

In order to avoid duplication and to increase efficiency, the cultural areas to be explored should be carefully matched with the available resources. When inviting an organization or agency spokesperson to speak to the inservice participants, a carefully prepared outline of areas to be covered should be given to this presenter well in advance of the session. The choice of topics should not be left to the speaker, who should be asked by the workshop leader which of the topics can be covered in the presentation. In this way, development of knowledge and understanding about an ethnic group is not left to chance.

Availability of presenters from or about ethnic groups may be dependent upon the size and concentration of the group in the community. Where there are sizable numbers of people, one tends to find more formal organizations which represent ethnic groups. These may range in purpose from ethnic advocacy to those whose sole function is to spread understanding and acceptance of the ethnic group through presentations of ethnic culture such as music, dance, art, foods, etc.

Another source of presenters would be governmental agencies in the community which have direct contact with the ethnic group being studied. If one agency cannot identify or provide speakers with first-hand contact and experience with the ethnic group being studied, it may be able to recommend another agency or office. Presenters should be sought who can provide the type of information about the ethnic group called for in the outline adopted for inservice study.

The two approaches previously mentioned—presenters from the ethnic group, and those from agencies serving the ethnic group—would appear to have the greatest potential for informing the inservice participants. Discrepant views may be expressed by various presenters, and these provide an opportunity for discussion and reconciliation of viewpoints. In situations and locations in which live speakers are unavailable, brief research papers or audio-visual presentations developed by individuals or groups within the inservice structure can be shared.

Additional knowledge without necessary adjustments in attitude will produce little change of the inservice group's behavior. As Jennifer E. Bahowick found in her study of school librarians in bilingual-bicultural programs, attitudes of school librarians were more important than lack of bilingual materials.[22] Bahowick reports that school librarians in a bilingual-bicultural education program interpreted their most important role with bilingual and limited-English-speaking students as that of helping the students to learn English and develop their reading skills in English. On the other hand, the bilingual coordinators thought libraries should help these students maintain pride in their own culture, help to develop a positive self-image, and learn about American culture and customs.[23]

A report by the Commission for Racial Equality (United Kingdom) cautions that education of librarians for a multicultural society, should not rely exclusively on information relayed through representative community organizations. They state that "there is no alternative to exhaustive local fieldwork."[24]

Of course, fieldwork is not always possible in an inservice situation, given time and other constraints, but, if it is possible, direct exposure to the ethnic group being studied can add much to each participant's understanding. Short-term service in a branch library located in the ethnic neighborhood being studied is a possibility for field study, or contacts made with ethnic group organizations or community agencies serving the ethnic group can be utilized for this experience. Even a few hours of direct contact can be beneficial for inservice participants. As the Commission for Racial Equality states, "The need for direct contact with minority group communities and organizations must be emphasized."[25]

Attention has been focused upon various avenues for learning about the culture of the ethnic group being studied. A combination of presentations from ethnic group organizations, governmental agencies, independent study, and fieldwork has been advocated. At some point, a decision must be made as to when sufficient information has been obtained by inservice participants so that some action can result from the new knowledge gained.

The tentative generalizations which have been drawn together by workshop experience need to be reexamined. In this experience, the group as a whole should reevaluate their list, deleting items, adding others, and correcting any distortions or misinformation. The final list of generalizations, especially those placed under the "action" heading, form the basis for the next phase of inservice training.

Assessing the Effectiveness of Present Library Programs for Ethnic Groups

A brief statement can serve as a guideline for assessing the effectiveness of library services to the ethnic group: "The good library should help to establish cultural identity and a good self-image for all children, particularly members of minority groups."[26]

The first response of many to the task of assessing current library services as related to the ethnic group being studied (Hispanic and / or Asian) may be to inspect the collection of materials relating to this ethnic group. Certainly, this is a good beginning, but a broader perspective should be adopted. There are several broad questions encompassing both services and materials: How has the library assisted members of the ethnic group in building and maintaining pride in their native culture? To what degree has the library assisted the ethnic group in learning about American culture and customs? And, most important to a new or recent immigrant population: how well has the library helped members of this group to cope with everyday life and its problems in a new culture?

There may be value in having a detailed checklist for each inservice participant to use for assessment, but such a list may be too comprehensive for small libraries and insufficient for large library systems. From a list of leading questions to act as springboards, additional criteria for assessment can be added.

Guide questions which can be used for assessment are:

1. To what extent do members of the ethnic group now utilize library services?
2. Which kinds of outreach efforts has the library made to encourage greater library usage and participation among members of the ethnic group?
3. What are the present attitudes of library personnel toward members of the ethnic group?
4. Which special events have been held at the library to help the ethnic group learn about and value their culture?
5. What special promotion (bulletin boards, display, etc.) has the library had to highlight the ethnic group and stimulate cultural appreciation for its food, arts, music, dance, literature, poetry?
6. What has been the leadership role of the library in highlighting the ethnic group or placing emphasis on the positive values of the multicultural characteristics of the community?
7. Which kinds of cooperative efforts has the library made with community ethnic social organizations in informing others about their cultural group?
8. How much effort has been made by the library to work cooperatively with governmental agencies in assisting the ethnic group?
9. Are there sufficient numbers and varieties of materials in both English and languages other than English which are of acceptable quality in the library collection to adequately serve the ethnic group?
10. Are there librarians or technical library assistants who are either members of the ethnic group or who speak their native language?
11. Have any community members of this ethnic group been involved in planning and / or carrying out any of the above activities?

Assessment of library services may be performed on an individual basis, or, if there are two or more employees from the same library, small groups may be formed for this activity. If sufficient time is spent in doing an honest and comprehensive assessment, the next step in the inservice training design will be more easily accomplished.

Library Service Programs for Ethnic Groups

The assessment activity should yield a mosaic of the efforts and types of activities which the library has used to relate to the ethnic group. A value judgement should be made to determine if the activities have been productive in terms of helping the ethnic group and / or helping the rest of the community to become informed about and to value the culture of the ethnic group. Library staff members who have been successful in providing services to an ethnic group should be encouraged to share "success stories" with the inservice group, with particular emphasis on activities which "work." Descriptions are needed with analyses of the reasons why these undertakings were successful. Knowing the success factors can help inservice participants to formulate activities in terms of the resources available to them. According to Juliana Bayfield, "The success of children's libraries for a multicultural population is dependent as much on the members of the staff as on the resources. Their motivation and ability to communicate with the public is of utmost importance."[7]

Rasmussen and Kolarik made the point that "Multiculturalism as a concept makes demands of the host society; it requires it 'to promote or even encourage some degree of cultural and social variation within an overall context of national unity'."[28] Helping immigrants to adapt to their new environment while retaining some sense of being rooted in their origin and heritage is the library's task — not an easy but a challenging and important one. The needs of adults as well as children must be considered and met. Making the ethnic community aware of the library's potential usefulness to its members as an information center can be in part accomplished through the use of ethnic radio / TV channels and the ethnic press, as well as through the visibility of a bilingual staff in places — such as shopping areas — where large numbers of the ethnic group gather.[29]

Areas of information commonly needed by most ethnic group adults, especially recent immigrants to this country, include coping information related to health, employment, finances, job training, and education.[30] New ways of shopping, cooking, and homemaking are of vital concern to many women who are trying to settle in to a new life.

Exhibits and cultural-heritage projects have been popular library activities for about two decades now. Like the Tulsa, Oklahoma, program which ran over a period of four months, and the Brooklyn, New York, program which ran for two years, these projects, undertaken with grant funds, are mounted for a limited period only, whatever period the funds cover, as a rule.[31] They are cited as being only two of many which featured drama, dance, folklore, music, poetry, painting, and other arts including cinema, cooking, discussions, exhibits, and displays. Dispite their relatively short duration, many have had lasting effects on their communities in terms of the ethnic groups highlighted and appreciation of them by the rest of the community. Evaluation documented that twenty thousand people were reached by the Tulsa program and that, since the project, there is much greater attendance at ethnic group celebrations, such as those of the Greek-Orthodox and Mexican-American communities.[32]

Some of the findings reported from evaluation of the Brooklyn program provide useful clues to success / failure factors for program planners:

1. Music and dance were the most popular of the programs, with poetry and film the least popular.
2. Group attendance is larger when arrangements are made for transportation.
3. Many who were attracted by this special programming were those who otherwise might not have utilized library services.
4. Attendance was also dependent upon the type of facilities, the hospitality of the library branch managers, and the amount of local publicity given.
5. "Intercultural experiences are most easily conveyed in nonverbal terms. Audiences empathized with music and dance from cultures other than their own much more easily than with literary expressions or lecture-type explanation of cultures."[33]

It should be noted that the majority of the cultural heritage programs sponsored by libraries, including those cited in Tulsa and Brooklyn, have been focused not on recent immigrant groups but rather on ethnic groups or minorities that have lived for a long time submerged and / or undervalued in the midst of the majority culture. Much of the focus has been on the black community, with activities spurred several times annually by such events as Black History Month (February) and Dr. Martin Luther King's birthday, in January (now a national legal holiday), which assure a certain amount of news coverage. Communities with substantially large ethnic or cultural minority populations—Greek, Polish or American Indian, for example—have highlighted these groups and their culture from time to time, sometimes on a fairly regular basis. The theme of immigration from other lands to America could well be used to weave together a program or series of programs tying the concerns and cultures of older immigrant groups to those of newer vintage, and could apply to all groups except, of course, the American Indians! (The Tulsa project featured American Indian culture, reflecting the large Indian population of Oklahoma.) Interestingly, the two cultural minority categories upon which this book is focused are characterized by including both very old immigrant groups to this country and very recent ones. Certain Hispanic and Asian groups have a long history of residence here. This phenomenon is discussed fully in chapters 3 and 4.

Earlier mention was made of the importance of taking into account the initial reluctance to use libraries of immigrants who have had no library experiences in their countries of origin. Bayfield reports some ways in which libraries in Australia work to overcome this reluctance. These include:

1. publicizing services through multilanguage pamphlets about the library and advertisements in ethnic newspapers and on ethnic radio.
2. encouraging parents or grandparents to use library services when they bring children on library visits.
3. hosting various events, as cooking demonstrations, national weeks, and storytelling, for local national groups.
4. providing reading and outreach programs for immigrants with books and other materials. Language cassettes produced in Australia in pamphlet / cassette form are used in schools.
5. employing a staff with a variety of language skills who can relate to immigrants. This is done in libraries in larger cities.[34]

Sweden has also designed some successful approaches for relating to the needs of immigrant children and encouraging children to read and to come to the library:

1. Children in nursery schools as well as elementary schools are taken to the library on a regular schedule.
2. Books are placed in locations for children's use in health clinics, immigrant association clubs, and in similar places.

3. Advertisements are placed in several languages in a Swedish immigrant journal.
4. Lists of materials in different languages are compiled.
5. Tapes with stories and folk music from their mother countries are available.
6. Film presentations for preschoolers are arranged.
7. Story hour for children (at one location available in eight different languages) is offered. Librarians in Stockholm found that children like to listen to stories in another language and then have them translated by other children who know the language.
8. An awareness in Swedish children of the problems faced by immigrant children who have other languages is developed by: (a) books about immigrant children; (b) books for children about the countries from which these children came; and (c) exhibitions of drawings by immigrant children on the theme of being a foreigner in Sweden.[35]

It should be noted that many of these services in the library are for all children in Sweden, with some special attention to the needs of immigrant children.

School librarians are afforded many opportunities to assist children in learning about and valuing ethnic groups — their own as well as others. The handbook for school librarians by Haley and others provide related activities:

1. Cultural-Awareness Week / Community Fair / Ethnic Day — use of ethnic costumes, dances, food, music, games, books and nonprint material exhibits, as well as other activities, are suggested.
2. Roots research / genealogy study — using such materials as *Finding Your Roots: How Every American Can Trace His Ancestors at Home and Abroad*, by Jeane Eddy Weston (New York: Ballantine Books, 1977), and *Family History for Fun and Profit*, by Vincent L. Jones and others (Salt Lake City, Utah: Publishers Press, 1972). Students are encouraged to trace their family histories.
3. Speakers — bring in ethnic speakers to talk about ethnic practices and customs in their families.
4. Bulletin boards — focus on different ethnic groups including art reproductions, ethnic customs, artifacts, and other items.
5. Displays — focus on a single theme, such as ethnic art, food, religion, or games, and display library materials including recordings filmstrips, art books, cookbooks, and fiction.

6. Local ethnic radio programs—inform students of the schedule and encourage them to listen.

7. Poetry readings—have students read and illustrate a favorite poem chosen from several anthologies representative of different ethnic groups.

8. Ethnic learning center—establish a small area of the library in which all kinds of library materials are kept that deal with ethnic groups.

9. Daily bulletin—place ethnic reminders of special days, such as holidays or days when special customs are observed.

10. Newsletter—send to faculty members and others an occasional newsletter describing new library materials about ethnic groups.

11. Oral history—use taped student interviews of parents, faculty, or community persons and photographs regarding ethnic heritage and customs and make these available in the library. A suggested guide is *You and Aunt Arie: A Guide to Cultural Journalism Based on "Foxfire" and Its Descendants*, by Pamela Wood. This is available as an ERIC document (ED 120 090) or from the Institutional Development and Economics Affairs Service, 1785 Massachusetts Avenue, N.W., Washington, D.C. 20036.

12. Field trips—sponsor field trips to local sites, such as cemeteries, historical centers, and others which yield information about ethnic heritage.

13. Personal resource file—develop a list of people representative of different ethnic groups who would be available as speakers to classes or guides on ethnic-related field trips. Make this list available to teachers.

14. Brown-bag lunch—sponsor a "brown-bag" lunch for students and invite community persons of different ethnic backgrounds to interact with the students.

15. Book talks—talk about folk tales from different countries and books dealing with ethnic groups.

16. Talent show—invite people representative of different ethnic groups to participate in a music and dance festival at the library.

17. Bookmarks—sell bookmarks made by the librarian or children which are decorated with traditional designs of different ethnic groups.

18. Get-to-Know-Your-Neighbor Week—encourage children to interview neighbors regarding ethnic backgrounds and use the informa-

tion to make a chart of the different ethnic groups represented in the school neighborhood.

19. Grandmother trunks — help children develop "grandmother trunks" packed with items such as clothing, artifacts, magazine articles, art, and books which are about different ethnic groups. The trunks may be used in the library or the classrooms.

20. Inservice workshop — conduct an inservice workshop on ethnic studies for faculty members. Recommended materials: the filmstrip "Ethnic Studies: What is an Ethnic Group?" produced by Educational Design, Inc. (47 West 13th Street, New York, N.Y. 10011). This filmstrip is part of the series "Ethnic Studies: The Peoples of America." Inform faculty members of available materials through an overview and opportunity to examine materials.[36]

A wide variety of sources has been utilized so that the reader is introduced to a number of activities and ideas which can be adapted to fit the situation in which that person is working. What is needed in one situation may be completely out of place in another. A wide selection of activities can be orchestrated into an ongoing program with a variety of approaches. There is no one best approach for all situations — nor even one best approach for one situation. A variety of activities reinforce one another.

Another consideration should be kept in mind: libraries do not have to work independently of other community agencies and services. Cooperative efforts with universities, local schools, social agencies, ethnic organizations, and others can broaden the base for input of ideas, distribute efforts evenly, combine a greater number of resources, provide enough shared credit to go around, and possibly be more effective than "library only" efforts.

As part of the inservice training activities, participants should be encouraged to list organizations from which cooperation may possibly be secured, and advised how to contact and work with them. Roles must be clearly defined in terms of the overall effort and should be determined through joint efforts of the library and the organizations involved. The library program and activities selected to serve and / or highlight the ethnic group should be developed with flexibility, subject to refinement or revision. Provision for input by interested organizations into the library's program is a must and will help to insure the sustained efforts and cooperation of these organizations.

Evaluating the Effectiveness of Programs

Library programs which seek to improve services to the ethnic group must be evaluated at appropriate intervals during the process of development as well as at the end of them. Certainly, summative (or final) evaluation is necessary, but formative (or ongoing) evaluation, done during the course of the project or program, allows for adjustment so that components which are not productive are identified and can be modified or changed to improve a project while it is still in progress.

Suppose, for example, that several programs have been held in the library aimed at increasing cultural appreciation of a particular ethnic group, and these programs have been poorly attended. Appraisal of this situation would examine the program, publicity for it, appeal to the target group, library atmosphere and hospitality, and degree of cooperation with ethnic or community organizations, among other factors affecting attendance. Based on the evaluator's findings, changes should be recommended to improve attendance. By making evaluation a continuous concern, the number of unproductive efforts can be reduced.

As was previously mentioned in this chapter when assessment of library services was discussed, the criteria by which a library judges the effectiveness of its service to a particular ethnic group are highly individual ones. Some indicators of increased effectiveness of service to an ethnic group will appear in a short time; others will not become apparent immediately, but will be measured over a longer period.

As Bayfield says about the challenge of multicultural library service to children, "Australia in the 1980s is being faced with the same challenges to its economy as those of any other highly industrialized nation. Inflation is causing cutbacks in public spending and the growing use of technology in private industry and the public services is bringing hardship to a greater number of people. In times such as these, public libraries have an even more vital part to play in people's welfare."[37] The challenges and opportunities for libraries in the United States are no less.

PART 2
INTRODUCTION

The United States of America is a land of immigrants. The struggles of these groups of immigrants with economic hardship, ethnic stereotyping, outright discrimination, and the clashes between new-and old-world values are well-documented parts of our history. The early and predominantly Caucasian immigrants were, for the most part, from Europe. Members of another racial group, many forcibly removed from their homelands, were from Africa.

But the United States can no longer be thought of as a two-race society. In recent years, new immigrations have permanently changed both the racial and ethnic composition of this country. The high birthrate of Spanish-origin people living in the United States, coupled with legal and illegal immigration from Mexico and Central and South American countries, are increasing their numbers so rapidly that it is predicted that by the year 2020 this group will become our largest cultural minority, accounting for 15 percent of the population.[1]

Another group, East Asians, has increased in dramatic fashion. In 1970, East Asians comprised only about three quarters of one percent of the population. During the decade of the '80s, their total number more than doubled with the arrival of 1,312,000 immigrants. The 1980 census shows 3,500,000 people of East Asian origins in this country, which includes approximately 1.5 percent of the total population. In 1981, for example, 213,000 East Asians came to live in America.[2]

Predictions of future immigration to the United States show a decline of people from European countries and a continuation of the large numbers of East Asians (particularly Southeast Asians) and those from Spanish-origin countries, seeking refuge in a land that promises both freedom and opportunity.

The changing racial and ethnic composition of America will not come about through the "melting-pot" approach by which immigrants were to be socialized through the schools and other societal forces, giving up their old-world identity and replacing it with the values, perceptions, and customs of the new country. This version of "Americanizing" immigrants left many casualties among immigrant groups.

The new version of acculturation embraces cultural pluralism. This concept holds that one does not have to surrender ethnic and cultural identity in order to become an American. With this approach, one views America through more realistic lenses, ground to a prescription comprised of many diverse ethnic and cultural groups. The pluralistic view recognizes that the strength of America is in its cultural diversity, and that this diversity should be not denied but valued.[3]

Recommendations for the suggested readings which follow the background descriptions of selected cultures in chapters three and four are, in many instances, those provided by authorities in the study of those cultural groups. Older essential titles have been included, as well as newer ones, in some of the lists. The notes about many of these publications are those of the authorities consulted. Older titles may not show up on other lists. In other cases, both bibliographies and individual titles were examined by the authors and briefly annotated, and some titles were listed as recommended but without annotations.

The intention of the authors has been to provide information in an easy to use form. Titles vary in many regards: some are starting points for teachers and librarians little acquainted with a given culture; others assume a greater degree of knowledge. Some titles contain information about several cultures, but have been listed only in the section on one of them. Therefore it may be useful for the reader to skim lists provided under several cultures other than just the one being considered. The bibliographical information provided in the List of Background Readings includes some addresses which would ordinarily not appear in a bibliography in an attempt to assist those looking for resources who may wish to acquire certain titles.

Chapter 3
Backgrounds of Hispanic Children and Young People in the United States

HISPANIC PEOPLE IN THE UNITED STATES

Terminology makes difficult the description of a population as diverse as this one. The terms *Hispanic, Spanish-origin, Spanish-speaking, Hispano, Hispanic Americans, Spanish-Americans, Latin-Americans*, and others have been used by various writers. Of the terms mentioned, the first three are those in more popular usage. The terms Hispanic and Spanish-origin are used by writers of government documents. Spanish-speaking lacks accuracy, because not all households so denoted employ Spanish as their usual language. Some Hispanic groups speak the Spanish language in 96 percent of the households (Cubans), while others reach a high of 75 percent (those from Central or South America). Overall, 80 percent of Hispanic persons live in households where Spanish is spoken.[1]

The Spanish-origin group can be divided into subgroups, the largest being Mexican Americans, who comprise approximately 60 percent of all Hispanic Americans in the United States. Other Spanish-origin subgroups include Puerto Ricans, Central or South Americans, Cubans, and "other Spanish."[2]

It should be noted that almost 75 percent of all Hispanics live in five states: California, Texas, New York, Florida, and Illinois. Other states with high concentrations of Hispanic populations include New Jersey, New Mexico, Arizona, and Colorado. This is shown in Table 1.[3]

Table 1
Nine States with the Greatest Percentage of Hispanic Residents

State	1970	1980	% of 1980 Hispanics in USA
California	2,369,292	4,544,331	31.1
Texas	1,840,648	2,985,824	20.4
New York	1,351,982	1,659,300	11.4
Florida	405,036	858,158	5.9
Illinois	393,204	635,602	4.4
New Jersey	288,488	491,883	3.4
New Mexico	308,340	477,222	3.3
Arizona	264,770	440,701	3.0
Colorado	225,506	339,717	2.3

Source: Census Bureau

Although every state has some Hispanic residents, Hispanics account for 36 percent of the total population of New Mexico and 21 percent of the population of Texas.[4] Mexican Americans, the largest Hispanic group, are concentrated in the Southwest, reflecting the early colonization by Spain. Because of the availability of manufacturing and agricultural jobs, migrants of Mexican descent and Puerto Rican origin have been attracted to Illinois.[5] Urban Puerto Ricans are concentrated particularly in New York and New Jersey because of the high degree of industrialization in these states. Cuban Americans reside in the South, with the main concentration in Florida.[6]

The initial settlement patterns of the earlier immigrants would seem to be one of the many bases for population concentrations. Added to this are economic considerations, such as, available employment and the location of the states where they entered the United States.

According to federal government sources, more than half (51.1 percent) of the Spanish-origin population in the U.S. lives in central cities.[7] Hispanics comprise 6 percent of the total U.S. population.[8] This amounts to 15.2 million people. Many believe that this seriously undercounts the population because of the high number of illegal Hispanic immigrants, an estimated 680,000 undocumented Mexicans alone having entered the United States in 1975.[9]

Important Facts

Hispanics in the United States are younger than blacks or whites, with a median age of 23. The median age for blacks is 25, as compared to 31.5 for whites.[10]

Approximately two-thirds of the Hispanic group's population increase can be attributed to high fertility coupled with death rates comparable to those of other ethnic groups. The fertility rate is 2.5 births for each Hispanic woman in the United States, compared to 1.8 for other women.[11]

Since 1960, Hispanics have averaged 40 percent of the total immigration to the United States. It is predicted that by 2020, Hispanics will total 47 million, accounting for 15 percent of the United States population.

Hispanics will be stronger politically in future years. At the present time, the governor of New Mexico is Hispanic, as are the mayors of Denver, Miami, and San Antonio, as well as nine United States congressmen. Hispanics want to assimilate into the United States but still retain a strong cultural links with the past.

Problems of English language proficiency account for part of the reason Hispanics tend to be found in low-paying and semi-skilled jobs. Although Hispanics are known as good workers and their median family income is greater than that of blacks, but less than for whites, their educational achievement lags. In 1981, 72 percent of white males had completed four years of high school, compared to 53 percent for black males and 46 percent for Hispanic males.

The poverty rate of one-in-four for Hispanics is less than the one-in-three rate for blacks. For whites, a one-in-ten rate is found.[12]

Hispanics have larger families than do other Americans. While 81.7 percent of non-Hispanic families consist of four or fewer persons, the Hispanics in this category comprise 69.5 percent. Families consisting of six or more members describe nearly 16 percent of Hispanics, more than double the percentage for non-Hispanic families. Larger family size is found among Mexican Americans, with the smallest among Cubans and "other Hispanics" (countries of Central and South America, particularly the Dominican Republic, Columbia, Argentina, Ecuador, Nicaragua, and El Salvador).[13]

In 1976, approximately 6 percent (three million) of the total public school population on the elementary and secondary levels consisted of Hispanics. About two-thirds of these students were attending schools composed primarily of minority children. Dropout rates were considerably higher for Puerto Ricans and Mexicans Americans, compared to the other Hispanic subgroups.[14]

Other Hispanic People

In addition to those major Hispanic groups previously discussed, a number of others exist which share common elements, yet are distinct in their own ways.

Spanish. Since 1820, approximately 250,000 immigrants have come to the United States from Spain. Many have settled in urban areas, finding employment in skilled or semi-skilled occupations. Generally, they have kept to themselves. Although they speak the same language and have the same religion, they do not usually interact with other Hispanic groups.[15]

One subcultural group from mainland Spain is the Basque people, who numbered between ten and fifteen thousand and settled in such states as Oregon, Idaho, Wyoming, Colorado, Nevada, and California. Arriving in the nineteenth century, this group came as sheepherders and gradually dominated the sheep industry, including the support services of transportation and marketing. Basques survived the disputes with cattlemen over land-grazing rights and the negative "dirty foreigner" labels. They contributed to the development and economy of the West.[16]

Dominicans. In 1975, a total of 12,526 people from the Dominican Republic emigrated to the United States. Fleeing from poverty in their homeland, they came hoping for a better life. Because they lack marketable skills, and because of the racial prejudice accorded dark-skinned people, they have a high rate of unemployment. Living in poor urban environments, these families suffer from the value clashes and family disruptions common to many Spanish-speaking immigrants.[17]

Other Latin Americans. Colombia, Ecuador, and El Salvador are the next largest sources of Hispanic immigrants. It is estimated that over 300,000 Colombians live in the United States, many of them illegal aliens. Overpopulation and poverty motivate many of these people from Central and South America to seek residence in this country. Those who are here illegally tend to live a rather guarded existence, preferring large urban areas, such as New York City.

MEXICAN AMERICANS

The largest and oldest of the Hispanic groups in the United States is that of the Mexican Americans. Except for Native Americans, no other ethnic group can claim longer residence in this country, stretching back over four centuries.[18] As George I. Sanchez states: "Many times I have pointed out that the Mexican American is not an immigrant. As an Indian, the Southwest has been his home from time immemorial. As a Spaniard, borrowing the phrase from Will Rogers, he could have sent a committee to welcome John Smith to Jamestown."[19]

Early inhabitants were located mainly in the Southwest, in what are now the states of New Mexico, Texas, Colorado, Arizona, and California. Until 1848, all of this area formed the northern provinces of Mexico.[20] The ancestors of a few present-day Mexican Americans settled the vast regions of the Southwest, and one need only look at the names of older cities and towns to grasp the scope of their influence. Of the present Mexican American population most came as immigrants from Mexico.[21]

Because of the strong ties to Mexico in the past and the continuing relationships that exist for Mexican Americans, it is appropriate to examine briefly their unique culture and history. By 1521, after two years of stubborn resistance, Cortés, a Spanish explorer, conquered the Aztecs in Mexico and, with his army, took command of land stretching from the southern-most tip of South America to the southwest of the United States. Unlike English colonists, who brought their wives and considered themselves permanent settlers, the Spaniards were adventurers looking for gold and treasures.[22]

It is estimated that 300,000 Spaniards came to Mexico during the first three centuries of settlement. Because they brought few women with them, many married or lived with Indian women and created a new nationality in the Americas. Although the biological, linguistic, and cultural heritage of the Mexican Americans is primarily Spanish and Indian, there is some African influence also. Africans, called Moors, came with the Spanish to the Americas. Nearly 200,000 African slaves were also brought to Mexico and by 1900 were so thoroughly mixed with Indians and Spaniards that they were no longer identifiable as a separate racial group. The biological heritage of the Mexican is much more Indian than Spanish. As the ruling group, the Spaniards imposed their religion and culture on the Indian nations, but many elements of the Indian culture survived and exerted a strong influence on Mexican culture. [23]

The end of Spanish rule in 1821, continuing political struggles, and the sparsely populated provinces of northern Mexico (now our Southwest) contributed to dramatic changes. The Texas Revolution, in 1835, coupled with the United States annexation of Texas, in 1845, led to the Mexican-American War of 1846. [24]

In 1848, the United States and Mexico signed the Treaty of Guadalupe Hidalgo, in which Mexico lost, and the United States acquired, one-half of Mexico's territory. At the time of the signing of the treaty, there were 73,500 Mexicans in the Southwest, and these were guaranteed their language, religion, and culture, as well as all the land rights that could be proved by Spanish grant. Less than half of this land was confirmed and was thus lost. These people were to become United States citizens if they did not leave the area within one year. During that period, fewer than 2,000 returned to Mexico. [25]

In a short time, these Mexican Americans changed from majority population status to that of a minority. The Southwest was infused with Eastern capital, and railroads were built. Thousands of Anglo-Americans arrived to take up residence or work the mines for gold or silver. [26] Intermarriages were common.

The annexation of Mexican territory was completed when a survey showed that the line described in the Treaty of Guadalupe Hidalgo was based on a map that was inaccurate. Because the Mexican government was in need of money, 45,532 square miles of Mexican territory below Arizona were acquired in 1853 by the efforts of James Gadsen. [27] It is interesting to note that the first constitution of the state of California, created, in part, by people of Mexican background, established California as a bilingual state, remaining such until 1878. [28] In time, however, Anglo-Americans tended to dominate the Southwest, gradually pushing persons of the Mexican culture aside and transforming bilingual social institutions, such as schools, into places where only the English language was spoken. New buildings were built with "Eastern" character, as native values expressed in architecture were rejected. However, by the 1890s, through the efforts of tourists and writers, a "Spanish" cultural revival had begun which included efforts to restore the decaying missions of the Southwest and revive architectural styles. This renewal of interest, however, did not include the region's Mexican-Indian heritage. [29]

The Reclamation Act of 1902 brought irrigation and reclamation projects to the Southwest, and with them the need for unskilled labor, as thousands of Mexicans poured across the border.[30] The industrial and agricultural development of this region was furthered by the labor of Mexicans and Mexican Americans. With the 1910 political revolution in Mexico, the number of immigrants to the Southwest increased as it did again during World War I and the 1920s. By 1923 the border patrol was established in an effort to stem the tide of illegal entrants from Mexico. With the border long and difficult to police, and the opportunity to earn in three months in the United States what could be earned in a year in their homeland, eager Mexicans crossed the border to fill agricultural laborers' jobs in the United States. It is estimated that between 1914 and 1954, 2,500,000 Mexicans entered the United States. Of this number 750,000 remained permanently.[31]

These hundreds of thousands of new Mexican Americans had overcome many obstacles as they sought to improve their standard of living, but they found that "Anglo-Americans were prejudiced against people who were largely of native American, brown-skinned origin, who were poor, who of necessity lived in substandard or self constructed homes, who could not speak English, and who were not familiar with the workings of a highly competitive and acquisitive society."[32] Other reports attest to the degree of discrimination, stereotyping, and low class status suffered by Mexican Americans. Discrimination in the Southwest manifested itself in the form of "lack of job opportunity, lack of educational opportunity, segregation in housing, lack of equality before the law, and various kinds of social discrimination."[33] Even after Mexican Americans had established stable communities in the Southwest and even though many had served in the armed forces during World War II, degrees of misunderstanding and lack of acceptance continued. Many Mexican Americans were decorated for bravery in World War II, and eleven received the Congressional Medal of Honor.[34]

Acceptance and respect gained momentum during and following the civil rights movement, but, despite these gains, progress in these matters has been slow and erratic. One writer states that few of the present-day residents of the Southwest realize that the conflict of cultures in the borderlands has raged for more than a century. He further states that Mexicans are a "conquered" people whose culture, character, and achievement as a people have been constantly deprecated.

This same writer states, "One of the first conditions to an improvement in Anglo-Hispanic relations in the Southwest is . . . to give back to the Indio-Hispanic citizens the heritage of racial pride of which we have robbed them and to teach Anglo-Americans to respect and honor this heritage.[35]

Although as a group Mexican Americans have much in common with each other, there are also divisions in terms of values, customs, and aspirations. There is economic (or social-class) diversity among them, and ranges in occupation from professional to migrant worker. Degree of acculturation and integration into the mainstream of society is yet another dimension. Another classifying consideration is the degree of Caucasian ancestry they possess or whether they object to being called "Mexicans" and prefer the term "Spanish-American."[36]

There are many more distinctions, of course, but what of the ties that bind this group and give them common identity and purpose? Pride in being of Mexican background and heritage is an uniting factor which is maintained through folk-level educational agencies (benevolent societies, patriotic organizations, and the extended family). This pride of background receives further reinforcement through Spanish-language radio and television programs, newspapers, and magazines, as well as Mexican-American political organizations. Maintaining a sense of belonging and cultural identity through these various influences also includes assimilating new cultural influences from Mexico. Pride in the Spanish language, Mexican arts and crafts, music, dancing, cooking, family structure, and the sense of community are thus preserved.[37]

As young people of Mexican American heritage come under the influence of schools and other social organizations of primarily "Anglo" orientation, there is some concern that instead of becoming bicultural (fully functional in their own as well as the larger mainstream culture), they become marginal to both groups. Confusion about self-identity can easily arise, so that no firm value base is constructed. Some extremely valuable Mexican traits should not be lost if one is to become truly bicultural. These include "the strong extended family, the tendency towards mutual aid, the Spanish language, artistic and musical traditions, folk dances, fine cooking and such personality characteristics as placing more emphasis upon warm interpersonal relationships than upon wealth acquisition."[38]

Many majority society (Anglo) citizens have failed to give proper recognition and credit to the hard-working builders who were the ancestors of contemporary Mexican Americans. Their contributions in terms of foods, customs, art, music, dancing, and language are readily acknowledged, but seldom their substantial roles in the economic development of the Southwest, which was, in fact, made possible through labor provided by Mexicans and Mexican Americans.

Other important contributions have often been lost in the pages of history books. One of the most colorful eras of American history is that of the cowboy. Somehow, it is rarely mentioned that everything the American cowboy used, including utensils, language, methods, and equipment, was adapted from their associations with the *vaquero* (or Mexican cowboy). Examples (and there are many) include the lasso, cinch, halter, chaps, stirrup tips, feed bag, rope halter, ten-gallon hat, roping, and horsebreaking techniques. Even the branding of cattle and the idea and method of brand registration is of Spanish / Mexican origin.[39]

Cattle raising, a big industry in the western United States, can trace its beginnings from cattle brought to the Southwest by Coronado, a Spanish adventurer. Sheep raising and wool production are Spanish / Mexican contributions which had their beginnings in New Mexico. Not only were sheep brought to the Southwest, but the Navajos and others were taught the processing and dyeing of wool. The mule industry, which was strong for many years in Missouri, is another Spanish / Mexican contribution. Early irrigation methods that transformed the arid desert lands of the Southwest to rich agricultural ground were based on Mexican methods, which were taught to the Mexicans by the Spaniards.[40]

Another important contribution, which has aided the rights of women for years, is the right of community property, which is based on Spanish law. This legacy of the Southwest, which recognizes the economic contributions of a wife during a marriage, has been called "one of the most important landmarks of Spanish civilization in America."[41]

Not to be forgotten are the methods of mining that were used in the gold mines of California and the copper mines of Arizona. These, too, are of Mexican origin.[42]

The list of cultural contributions of Mexican Americans and their ancestors is long,[43] yet the respect and recognition they deserve has not been accorded them. Slowly, but all too slowly, gains are being made as more and more Mexican Americans move up the economic ladder. As more of them begin to interpret and understand the American dream, they wonder why it cannot be theirs.[44]

Background Readings: Mexican Americans[45]

North from Mexico: The Spanish-Speaking People of the United States, by Carey McWilliams is especially recommended. McWilliams gives an objective and clear historical account of Mexican Americans in the United States, from days preceding written historical documents through World War II.

Other recommended titles include:

Acuña, Rodolfo. *Occupied America: The Chicano's Struggle toward Liberation.*

Anaya, Rudolfo A. *Bless Me Ultima.*

Gomez, David. *Somos Chicanos: Strangers in Our Own Land.*

Grebler, Leo, Joan W. Moore, and Ralph C. Guzman. *The Mexican-American People: The Nation's Second Largest Minority.*

Meier, Matt S., and Feliciano Rivera. *The Chicanos: A History of Mexican-Americans.*

Meining, D. W. *Southwest. Three People in Geographical Change, 1600–1970.*

Moore, Joan W., with Alfredo Cuellar. *Mexican Americans.*

Moquin, Wayne, with Charles Van Doren, eds. *A Documentary History of the Mexican-Americans.*

Ortego, Philip D., ed. *We are Chicanos. An Anthology of Mexican-American Literature.*

Romano-V., Octavio I. "The Anthropology and Sociology of the Mexican-Americans."

_____. "The Historical and Intellectual Presence of Mexican-Americans."

Rosaldo, Renato, Robert A. Calvert, and Gustav L. Seligmann, eds. *Chicano: The Evolution of a People.*

Steiner, Stan. *La Raza: The Mexican-Americans.*

Stoddard, Ellwyn R. *Mexican-Americans.*

Tebell, John, and Ramon E. Ruiz. *South by Southwest: The Mexican-American and His Heritage.*

Weber, David J., ed. *Foreigners in Their Native Land: Historical Roots of the Mexican Americans.*

Although many of the materials listed above provide essential historical information, the examination of recent publications can provide additional insights about the history, literature, and concerns of Mexican Americans in various localities within the United States. Recent materials which relate to history include:

DeLeon, Arnoldo. *They Called Them Greasers: Anglo Attitudes toward Mexicans in Texas, 1821–1900.*

Martin, Patricia Preciado. *Images and Conversations: Mexican Americans Recall a Southwestern Past.*

Natella, Arthur A., Jr., comp. and ed. *The Spanish in America, 1513–1979: A Chronology and Fact Book.*

Romo, Ricardo. *East Los Angeles: History of a Barrio.*

Materials which are concerned with literature include:

Baker, Houston A., Jr., *Three American Literatures: Essays in Chicano, Native American and Asian American Literature.*

Keller, Gary D., and Francisco Jimenez, eds. *Hispanics in the United States: An Anthology of Creative Literature.*

Sommers, Joseph, and Thomas Ybarra-Frausto. *Modern Chicano Writers: A Collection of Critical Essays.*

Additional informative materials include:

Huerta, Jorge A. *Chicano Theater: Themes and Forms.*

Trejo, Arnulfo D., *The Chicanos: As We See Ourselves.*

Selected bibliographies to consult for additional background information include:

Foster, David William, ed. *Sourcebook of Hispanic Culture in the United States.* Contributors to this volume have developed essays, each of which indicates problems, controversies, and concerns in a specific discipline. Disciplines represented which relate to Mexican Americans include: history, anthropology, sociology, literature, and art. Annotated bibliographies follow each essay.

Hawkins, John N. *Teacher's Resource Handbook for Latin American Studies: An Annotated Bibliography of Curriculum Materials Preschool through Grade Twelve. This annotated list recommends audiovisual and printed materials for use with children and young people. A brief list of bibliographies and additional sources is provided. A list of publishers and distributors is given.*

Quintana, Helena, with the assistance of Richard Allen Moore, IV. *A Current Bibliography on Chicanos 1960–1973, Selected and Annotated.*

Current books on Chicanos which can be useful to teachers are listed and accompanied by descriptive annotations. Books considered classics which were published before 1960 are included, as is a representative selection of juvenile literature. Levels of recommendations are indicated for elementary through college levels. Lists of Chicano periodicals and publishers are provided.

Schon, Isabel. *A Bicultural Heritage: Themes for the Exploration of Mexican and Mexican-American Culture in Books for Children and Adolescents.* Selected reading lists with discussion of selected titles within each list are provided by grade levels K–2, 3–6, and 7–12 for the following topics: customs, lifestyles, heroes, folklore, and key historical developments. In appendix B, the lamentable lack of literature from Mexico for children and young adults is discussed: some authors and titles are discussed, and a selected reference list for adults is provided. In appendix C, the author advocates the inclusion of literature from Spain in collections for children and young people. Representative authors and titles are discussed.

Schon, Isabel. *A Hispanic Heritage: A Guide to Juvenile Books about Hispanic People and Cultures.* Information is provided about many in-print books in English published since 1979 in the United States. General books on Latin America are included.

Trejo, Arnulfo D. *Bibliografía Chicana: A Guide to Information Sources.* An annotated bibliography of bibliographies as well as individual titles on diverse topics is provided. Information about Chicano newspapers and periodicals is included. A directory of publishers is another useful aid.

The following core collection includes juvenile literature: *A Core Collection of Print Material for Libraries Serving the Spanish Speaking of the Southwest.* Compiled by the Arizona Chapter of REFORMA.

PUERTO RICANS

This is the second largest of the Hispanic groups in this country. Their origin in the United States has some similarity to that of Mexican Americans. Both groups were part of the territorial acquisition of this country following wars. In 1898 the Treaty of Paris, which followed the Spanish-American War, allowed the United States to acquire the Philippines, Puerto Rico, and American Guam.[46]

Spain had controlled the island of Puerto Rico for more than four hundred years (from 1493 to 1897), enslaving the people, making no improvements, concentrating the wealth in the hands of a few, perpetuating a high rate of illiteracy, and providing poor health facilities.[47] By 1777, the 40,000 native Taino Indians who had been peacefully engaging in farming, hunting, and raising animals when they were conquered by the Spanish were almost extinct in Puerto Rico. Some were killed in skirmishes with the Spaniards, others died of diseases brought by the invaders, and a few escaped to other islands.[48]

Slaves were brought in from Africa, so that, today, the major racial heritages of Puerto Ricans are Indian, African, and Spanish. The amalgamation of these strains is quite thorough, although it may be more desirable to be white (or light-skinned) in Puerto Rico, and whites are more likely to be members of the upper class. Social -class status is often as important as race. Banks points out that blacks in Puerto Rico can and do enter the upper class, and that when they do, their race is less important in social relationships.[49] Thus, being black in Puerto Rico is less a handicap than being black in the United States.

Though skin color is less important in Puerto Rico than in the United States, Puerto Ricans have a variety of designations of shades: blanco (white), prieto (dark-skinned), negro (black), and trigueño (tan) are some examples. Within a family, one may find individuals who are characterized as negro, blanco, and trigueño.[50]

The Jones Act of 1917 made Puerto Ricans citizens of the United States and subject to military draft.[51] Until 1947, the governor of Puerto Rico was appointed by the president of the United States, but since then, governors have been elected. After the election of Luis Muñoz Marin as governor, in 1948, Puerto Rico became a commonwealth in 1952, giving it some governmental autonomy yet maintaining ties with the United States.[52]

With this change of status, Muñoz attempted to diversify the economic base of Puerto Rico, so that in addition to reliance on the three main cash crops of sugar, tobacco, and coffee, industrialization was encouraged. A plan called "Operation Bootstrap" was mounted which encouraged American manufacturers to locate their operations in Puerto Rico. The attraction was a large base of cheap labor and tax exemptions for up to ten years. By 1977, 2,000 plants had been established, millions of dollars were invested, and the income from manufacturing was more than three times larger than that from agriculture.[53]

This move brought mixed blessings. The island's per capita income increased dramatically, but urban slums were created as poverty merely shifted from a rural setting. Some critics claim that although Operation Bootstrap created a middle class in Puerto Rico, it was of greatest benefit to the upper class and to American industrialists. Nevertheless, according to Parrillo, Puerto Rico, through Operation Bootstrap, became the most highly industrialized land in the Caribbean and in most of Central and South America, with per capita income higher than in the other areas.[54]

Unemployment in Puerto Rico, which has remained at a constant 12 percent since 1946, has been an important factor in encouraging migration to the mainland. When the mainland economy rises, creating jobs, the movement of Puerto Ricans to the United States increases also. The reverse also happens. The migration by air to the United States began in 1940 and has continued.

Reduction in the number of low-skill jobs and a rise in those requiring additional education and higher skills has made it more difficult in recent years for the average Puerto Rican to secure employment.[55] Low levels of schooling,[56] difficulty with the English language,[57] and racial and ethnic discrimination[58] pose sizable barriers for Puerto Ricans seeking employment in the United States.[59] These problems are further complicated by political activists demanding Puerto Rican independence from the United States. Political stresses, plus the impact of social and economic forces previously mentioned, pose serious problems for Puerto Ricans in their attempts to establish an identity and be upwardly mobile.

Although some Puerto Ricans assimilate and others attempt to live a bicultural life, many avoid cultural conflict by confining their activities mainly to the ethnic community. For immigrants of the past, retreat to the security of the family has been a haven, but for new Puerto Rican immigrants, the frequent instability of the family structure in the United States makes this difficult. Change in traditional family roles is a serious problem.[60]

With the increasing necessity of working wives in the United States and their increased independence, there is little support for the traditional *machismo* of the father role. Added to this are school and community values that teach that children should have more freedom. Legal support through the courts for women and children further undermines the total obedience to the man as head of family that immigrants bring from Puerto Rico.

For many years, most Puerto Rican immigrants lived in various parts of New York City.[61] Other major concentrations can now be found in Chicago, San Francisco, and Cleveland. Ethnic neighborhoods provide some shelter from the biting winds of cultural conflict. Here, Spanish can be spoken, ethnic foodstuffs purchased, herbs and plants for folk medicine obtained, and the familiar establishments of Puerto Rico found: bodegas, travel agencies, and storefront Pentecostal churches.

Community organizations which attempt to enrich the lives of Puerto Ricans on the mainland include Aspira, Puerto Rican Forum, Puerto Rican Community Development, and the Puerto Rican Family Institute. Athletic leagues, cultural organizations, social clubs, and parent-action groups can also be found in several communities.

Because of the legal action of Aspira of New York, Inc., in 1974, the New York City schools agreed to expanding bilingual-bicultural instruction provided to Puerto Rican students. Increased awareness of and participation in city and state elections by the Puerto Rican community in New York have indicated their growing importance in the electoral process.

Background Readings: Puerto Ricans[62]

The reading of *Family Installments: Memories of Growing Up Hispanic*, by Edward Rivera, is an ample reminder that cultural experiences differ within linguistic as well as cultural groups. Rivera describes his life experiences in a rural area of Puerto Rico and in New York City.

Readings recommended by Banks in *Teaching Strategies for Ethnic Studies* include: a treatment of contemporary problems, *Puerto Rican Americans: The Meaning of Migration to the Mainland*, by Joseph J. Fitzpatrick; an anthropological study, *Up From Puerto Rico*, by Elena Padilla; a historical study in both settings, *Puerto Rico and Puerto Ricans*, by Clifford A. Hauberg; and selections from varied sources in *The Puerto Rican Experience: A Sociological Sourcebook*, edited by Francesco Cordasco and Eugene Bucchioni. Three popular histories about life on Puerto Rico are recommended: *Puerto Rico: A Profile*, by Kal Wagenheim; *A Short History of Puerto Rico*, by Morton J. Golding; and *The Puerto Ricans: A Documentary History*, edited by Kal Wagenheim. A nationalistic interpretation is presented in *We, The Puerto Rican People*, by Juan Angel Silen. An additional selection is *Puerto Rico: Freedom and Power in the Caribbean*, by Gordon K. Lewis.

Recent publications which relate to the experiences of Puerto Rican Americans include:

Carrion, Arturo Morales, *Puerto Rico: A Political and Cultural History.*
Cordasco, Francesco, and Eugene Bucchioni, *The Puerto Rican Community and Its Children on the Mainland: A Source Book for Teachers, Social Workers and Other Professionals.*
Keller, Gary D., and Francisco Jimenez, *Hispanics in the United States: An Anthology of Creative Literature.*
Levine, Barry B. *Benjy Lopez: A Picaresque Tale of Emigration and Return.*
Mohr, Eugene V. *The Nuyorican Experience: Literature of the Puerto Rican Minority.*

A comprehensive guide to information about Puerto Ricans is *Puerto Ricans and Other Minority Groups in the Continental United States: An Annotated Bibliography*, edited by Diane Herrera, with a new foreword and supplemental bibliography by Francesco Cordasco, published in 1979. Although primarily concerned with Puerto Ricans on the United States mainland, some of the 2,155 entries (listed through December 1972) concern other Hispanics in the United States, and some information about American blacks and other minority groups is included.

Other recommendations in the *Interracial Books for Children Bulletin* include: *Puerto Rico and Puerto Ricans: Studies in History and Society*, edited by Adalbert Lopez and James Petras; and *Borinquen: An Anthology of Puerto Rican Literature*, edited by María Teresa Babín and Stan Steiner.

For organizations with limited funds, it is suggested in the bulletin that purchase be made of two paperback volumes about racism in the United States. This highly recommended title is *To Serve the Devil: A Documentary Analysis of America's Racial History and Why It Has Been Kept Hidden*, volume 1 and 2, by Paul Jacobs, Saul Landau, and Eve Pell.

CUBAN AMERICANS

In terms of numbers, Cubans are the third largest of the diverse Hispanic groups in the United States. Since the Spanish-American War (1898), the United States has had a direct relationship with Cuba, having secured Cuba's independence from Spain. It has, moreover, retained some control through the naval base at Guantanamo. For many years, Cuban immigrants to the United States were included with those from the West Indies, so that there is no accurate count from the early years of immigration.

Although a Cuban community in northern New Jersey dates back to 1850, Cuban immigrants did not arrive in large numbers until

1959.[63] The rise of the Castro regime led large numbers of Cubans to seek political asylum in the United States, ninety miles away. Many came with the hope that Castro would be overthrown eventually, and that they could then return to their homeland.

Cuban refugees of the '60s tended to be mostly middle and upper-class people with training and education in professional and technical fields. They arrived during the '60s and until 1973, by commercial airlines. After this period, with these flights cancelled, many attempts were made to reach the United States through small boats. By 1968, the number arriving in this manner was judged to be between ten and twelve thousand. It has been estimated that for one boat that was successful, three more were not, with tragic loss of lives.

The early Cuban immigrants were those who were most threatened by the revolution and had the financial means for escape. Even though many of these Cuban immigrants found that their professional training, education, and experience was not recognized in the United States, they were enterprising and determined; some middle-aged professionals even took jobs as unskilled workers. A number of wives found employment, so that by 1976, the Bureau of the Census showed the median income for Cubans to be above all other Hispanic groups, though still below the overall mean income in the United States. These industrious people were hailed as successful immigrants and viewed by some as a positive model for other Hispanic groups to emulate.[64]

A different kind of Cuban immigrant came to the United States in 1980, however. From a group of ten thousand who sought political asylum in the Peruvian embassy in Havana, and with permission to emigrate directly to the United States given by the Castro regime, their numbers, over a nine-day time period, swelled the immigration to 125,000. Boats were sent to Mariel, Cuba, to pick up these refugees, for whom President Carter had secured special immigration legislation. The Mariel boatlift contained a high proportion of black Cubans, single males, and blue-collar workers. Additionally, some (less than 5 percent) of these immigrants suffered from mental or physical problems or had committed serious crimes. Even though the Cuban community in Miami contributed over two million dollars in relief money, these refugees were relocated on military bases in Florida, Arkansas, Pennsylvania, and Wisconsin. Unlike the earlier immigrants, the Mariel-boatlift Cubans spent many months in fenced-in areas waiting for an organization or individual to sponsor their release. Violent outbreaks occurred at some camps after months of frustration. A year after their arrival, forty-five thousand Mariel Cubans were living below the poverty line in the United States, and their suicide rate was seven times the United States average.[65]

Negative attitudes towards the latest Cuban arrivals led voters in Dade County (Miami), in 1980, to approve a local antibilingual ordinance which disallowed the use of county taxes to promote any language other than English. This is somewhat surprising since approximately half of the county consisted of Cuban Americans by 1981. Although no Cuban American had ever been elected to any of the 160 seats in the Florida legislature, in 1981, Raul Martinez was elected mayor of Hialeah, Florida, a major Florida city.

Cuban immigrants suffer the common problems of cultural clash as do most other immigrants. The English language remains a barrier for some. Even with the addition of the Mariel boatlift immigrants, the Cuban group in the United States has an older average age than either Mexican Americans or Puerto Ricans.

Some problems of acculturation include increased freedom for females, especially daughters and working wives. The traditional Cuban custom accords much attention and respect to the aged. The fact that over 11,000 elderly Cubans in Dade County live alone is a problem for some. Others, who live with families, help with baby-sitting, allowing younger Cuban women to work.

In 1982, Cubans numbered 750,000 in this country, with the largest concentration in the Miami, Florida, area. New York City has a sizable Cuban population, as has the greater Los Angeles area.

Background Readings: Cuban Americans[66]

Although many materials are available about Cuba and the Cuban revolution, little has been published about Cuban experiences in the United States. A comprehensive history of Cuba is *Cuba — The Pursuit of Freedom*, by Hugh Thomas. It is available in Spanish. Information on Cubans in Miami, Florida, and their reasons for leaving Cuba is available in *Cubans in Exile*, by Richard R. Fagen, Richard A. Brody, and Thomas J. O'Leary. A descriptive account about how Cuba came to have Communist leadership is *Dagger in the Heart! American Policy Failures in Cuba*, by Mario Lazo.

In *A Handbook of American Minorities*, by Wayne Charles Miller, the following book by Rafael J. Prohlas and Lourdes Casal is identified as indispensable to the study of Cuban-Americans: *The Cuban Minority in the U.S.: Preliminary Report on Need Identification and Program Evaluation: Final Report for Fiscal Year 1973.* Bibliographical listings in English and Spanish are included in this study.

The following articles are recommended by Miller for the guidance they provide concerning literature: Lourdes Casal, "A Bibliography of Cuban Creative Literature: 1958–1971," "The Cuban Novel, 1959–1969, An Annotated Bibliography." Julio E. Hernandez Miyares, "The Cuban Short Story in Exile: A Selected Bibliography," Solomon Lipp, "The Anti-Castro Novel."

Naomi E. Lindstrom provides useful advice in "Cuban American and Continental Puerto Rican Literature," published in *Sourcebook of Hispanic Culture in the United States*, edited by David William Foster. Among the resources included in the annotated bibliography is an essay which is recommended as an extensive guide to Cuban exile prose fiction from 1960 to the early 1970s: Seymour Menton, *Prose Fiction of the Cuban Revolution.* Lindstrom identifies an important bibliographical source for persons interested in Cuban American writing: *Cuban Studies / Estudios cubanos.* Camelo Mesa-Lago, ed.

Additional publications which show several aspects of the lives of Cuban Americans include:

Boswell, Thomas D., and James R. Curtis. *The Cuban-American Experience: Culture, Images, and Perspectives.*

Fox, Geoffrey E. *Working-Class Emigrés from Cuba.*

Keller, Gary D., and Francisco Jimenez, *Hispanics in the United States: An Anthology of Creative Literature.*

Chapter 4
Backgrounds of East Asian Children and Young People in the United States

Although one of the most diverse of immigrant categories in the United States, Asian Americans have been treated as though they comprise a single group. Diversity should be considered in terms of national origin, location, customs, language, religion, politics, personality, physical characteristics, and subgroup differences. Asian immigrants to this country have shared the burden of severe racial discrimination and a generally negative image. Because of physical and cultural differences with the dominant Caucasian groups, they have been referred to as Orientals, a name which many consider an ethnic slur.

The 1980 census report shows that there were more than 3.5 million Asians and Pacific Islanders living in the United States, out of a total of 226,504,825 people.[1] Of the Asian groups, the largest are: Chinese (806,027), Filipinos (774,640), Japanese (700,747), and Koreans (354,529). Between 1970 and 1980, the number of Chinese, Filipinos, and Koreans increased substantially in the United States. Koreans, for example, increased from 69,130 to 354,529 during this period. In 1979, the largest of the Asian American groups was the Japanese. With the 1980 census count, they are now the third largest group. Since 1970, Filipinos have been the next largest group of immigrants, second only to Mexicans.

Since 1970, almost two million Asians have immigrated to the United States.[2] These include Laotians, Thais, Malaysians, Cambodians,

East Indians, Pakistanis, and Vietnamese. The number of Vietnamese in the United States in 1980 was 261,714. Figures provided by the U.S. Office of Refugee Resettlement for the year 1981 show the following numbers: Vietnamese (322,000), Laotian (141,000), Kampuchean (Cambodians) (102,000) and others (300,000).[3]

CHINESE AMERICANS

Gold in the California mountains was the lure that attracted the first Asian immigrants to the United States, beginning in 1848. From the three who started this odyssey, thousands more followed, reaching the peak immigration period in the 1870s, with twenty thousand in 1873 and almost twenty-three thousand in 1876.[4]

Their hardships were many. Most of the men, young and married, were forced to leave their wives and children behind and borrow money, at high rates of interest, for the passage. Many of the initial immigrants were from the district of Toishan, in the South China province of Kwangtung. Because of strong family and village ties, a large portion of their earnings were sent home.

Almost from the time they arrived, Chinese immigrants were subject to racial hostility, despite the desperate need for manual labor in the mid-nineteenth century. Often, they were forced out of "mining camps, forbidden to enter schools, denied the right to testify in court, not allowed to obtain citizenship, and even occasionally murdered."[5] "Whites thought that the Chinese were strange because of their traditional Chinese clothing, language, queues hairstyle (which whites called pigtails), and skin color."[6]

Many of the early immigrants, because of the shortage of women in California, took jobs normally reserved for women: cooking, laundry work, and domestic service. Later, however, most of the immigrants found employment as laborers. In 1860, the proportion of Chinese men to Chinese women in the United States was 95 to 5 percent. Working in gangs, Chinese laborers helped to build the western portion of the transcontinental railroad. The Chinese eventually comprised 90 percent of the workers on the Central Pacific Railroad, one of the two companies to complete the transcontinental railway in 1869.

During the building of the railroad, wartime demands on Eastern industries and the high cost of transporting Eastern goods resulted in the hiring of Chinese in the textile industry. With the ending of the

Civil War and the completion of the railroad, a surplus of labor resulted. This led to the racist antagonism by laborers, union organizers, and others against their competitors—Chinese laborers. Worsening economic conditions intensified the racist feelings and reinforced the negative stereotypes about Chinese sanitation and life styles. An anti-Chinese movement began in California and spread to other Western states. Not only were many discriminatory laws passed, including the Queues Ordinance, the Laundry Ordinance, and the Foreign Miner's Tax, but outright violent physical attacks were made on defenseless Chinese men, women, and children.[8]

By 1882, the Exclusion Law, enacted through federal legislation, suspended immigration of all Chinese laborers to the country for ten years.[9] Even though there was a change in 1924, the immigration law provided no quota for races ineligible for naturalization, which included Asians. Although periodically previewed, the exclusion laws remained in force until 1943.

By far the greatest percentage of Chinese immigrants since 1945 has been female. Factors such as revolution and the change in Chinese mainland government caused a large migration of wives and families. The War Brides Act of 1945 and the G.I. Finances Act of 1946 enabled Chinese women to immigrate as wives or fiancées of American G.I.'s Finally, the McCarren-Walter Act of 1952 allowed spouses and children of United States citizens to immigrate on a non-quota basis. While most of the early Chinese immigrants to the United States were here on a temporary basis, the later arrivals have come on a more permanent basis.

The establishment of Chinese families has led to a more traditional existence in the United States. As American-born Chinese move into the mainstream, fewer Chinatowns are surviving, with many being razed as part of the urban renewal movement. However, in Los Angeles, New York, and San Francisco, where Chinatowns are still considered important tourist attractions, they remain. Newly arrived immigrants from Hong Kong and China tend to live in Chinatown areas.

In spite of discrimination faced by Chinese Americans, their achievements in the areas of education, science, and the arts have been great. One study in 1969 showed that 17.1 percent were employed in professional and technical occupations, while only 4 percent were employed as laborers.[10] About 95 percent of Chinese Americans live in urban areas.

The Immigration Act of 1965, which liberally increased Asian immigration quotas, has been instrumental in increasing the Chinese population in the United States. It is interesting to note that between 1970 and 1980, the white American population increased by 6 percent, while the Chinese population in the United States increased 85 percent, to make it the largest of all Asian groups in this country.

Background Readings: Chinese Americans[11]

To obtain a content background about a given Asian people, Banks advocates, in *Teaching Strategies for Ethnic Studies*, that an individual book be read on each Asian American group. A recommended 1981 history is *The Chinese of America*, by Jack Chen. Recommendations by Banks include a technical work on Chinese and Japanese Americans, *The Asian in the West*, by Stanford M. Lyman; and comprehensive titles on Chinese Americans: *The Chinese in the United States*, by Rose Hum Lee; *Chinese in America Life: Some Aspects of Their History, Status, Problems and Contributions*, by Shien-woo Kung; *Chinese Americans*, by Stanford M. Lyman.

A popular treatment recommended by Miller in *A Handbook of American Minorities*, as well as by Banks, is *The Story of the Chinese in America*, by Betty L. Sung. Both Miller and Banks mention a documentary history of the persecutions endured by the Chinese in the United States: *"Chink!": A Documentary History of Anti-Chinese Prejudice in America*, edited by Cheng-Tsu Wu, which also records prejudices among some of the Chinese.

As a best introduction to Chinese American literature as well as Japanese American and Filipino American Literature, Miller recommends *Aiiieeeee! An Anthology of Asian-American Writers*, edited by Frank Chin, Jeffrey Paul Chan, Lawson Fusao Inada, and Shawn Hsu Wong. Another recommendation in terms of East-West culture is *Chinese Mother Goose Rhymes*, by Robert Wyndham. The vertical format contains traditional Chinese rhymes, riddles, and games enhanced with color illustrations.

A sociological study that details various aspects of Chinese American life is *The Challenge of the American Dream: The Chinese in the United States*, by Francis L. K. Hsu. Miller indicates that differences among contemporary groups of Chinese Americans, descriptions of Chinese religious groups, and patterns of friendship and hospitality, as well as problems related to adolescent behavior, are among the topics presented by Hsu.

Although the previous recommendations include basic historical accounts, recent publications about the history, literature, and educators of Chinese Americans, and in some instances other Asian Americans, include:

Dicker, Laverne Mau. *The Chinese in San Francisco: A Pictorical History*.
Glick, Clarence E. *Sojourners and Settlers: Chinese Migrants in Hawaii*.
Kim, Elaine H. *Asian American Literature: An Introduction to the Writings and Their Social Context*.
Nakanishi, Don T., and Marsha Hirano-Nakanishi, eds. *The Education of Asian and Pacific Americans: Historical Perspectives and Prescriptions for the Future*.
Quan, Robert Seto, with Julian B. Roebuck. *Lotus among the Magnolias: The Mississippi Chinese*.
Steiner, Stan. *Fusang, The Chinese Who Built America*.
Wu, William F. *The Yellow Peril: Chinese Americans in Fiction, 1850–1940*.

JAPANESE AMERICANS

The first Japanese immigrants were brought to Hawaii in 1868 by a British ship. Only 149 in number, they worked as contract laborers on the plantations. By 1870, there were only fifty-five persons of Japanese ancestry in the United States. It was not until 1886, however, that the Japanese government legalized immigration. By 1920 there were 111,010 persons of Japanese ancestry in this country. Peak periods of immigration were between 1891 and 1924, with about 200,000 persons coming during this period.[12]

Passage of the Chinese Exclusion Act of 1882 had stopped Chinese immigration, creating a need for farm laborers in the developing West. This void was filled by Japanese immigrants. They also worked in lumber mills, canneries, on the railroads, and in gardening and other industries.

As more and more Japanese immigrants became tenant farmers or small landowners, their industriousness and knowledge of cultivation placed them in serious competition with native farmers. By 1913 the first alien land-holding law was passed in California, which prohibited any person ineligible for citizenship from owning land and permitted such persons to lease land for no more than three years. The United States Naturalization Act of 1790 had made citizenship available only to free white aliens. In 1868 this law was modified to include persons of African descent (ex-slaves), but the Japanese were still excluded.[13]

Since children of Japanese immigrants were automatically U.S. citizens, the Japanese held land in their children's names. By 1920, California passed a law prohibiting aliens from being guardians of the property of minors or from leasing any land. The U.S. Supreme Court upheld this law in 1923, and New Mexico, Arizona, Louisiana, Montana, Idaho, and Oregon passed similar laws.

Other anti-Asian forces were at work in the schools. In 1906, the San Francisco school board passed a resoultion transferring ninety-three Japanese children who were scattered throughout the district's twenty-three schools into a segregated "Oriental" school in Chinatown.[14] This incident made national headlines and had international implications. Japan, which had defeated Russia in 1905 and made other nations aware of their growing military power, pressured Pres. Theodore Roosevelt to intervene. Under threat of a federal lawsuit, the school board rescinded its resolution. However, Roosevelt also issued an executive order barring entry into the mainland United States of Japanese immigrants from a bordering country or U.S. territory. This order was in effect until 1948. In addition to this, the so-called Gentlemen's Agreement of 1908 with Japan agreed to restrict, but not eliminate, the issuance of passports.

One loophole of the Gentlemen's Agreement was that it allowed wives of Japanese immigrants living in the United States to enter. Marriage by proxy permitted entrance of several thousand Japanese wives per year until World War I, and almost six thousand a year after the war.

Anti-Japanese forces rejoiced with the passing of the Immigration Act of 1924, which fixed quotas for south, central and eastern European countries on the basis of percentages of their emigrants living in the United States and prohibited immigration of aliens ineligible for citizenship. This, in effect, stopped Asian immigrants and remained in effect until 1952.

So successful were Japanese immigrants in the United States, despite the large discriminatory barriers, that by 1941 they raised 42 percent of California's truck crops.[15] They produced 90 percent of the state's peppers, strawberries, celery, and snap beans, as well as a large percentage of California's cucumbers, tomatoes, cabbage, carrots, lettuce, and onions.[16]

With the 7 December 1941 attack of Pearl Harbor by Japan, smoldering anti-Japanese sentiment was rekindled in the United States. Led by California farmers and politicians, rumors of fifth-column and espionage activities among Japanese in the United States were spread. Panic, distrust, and fear led to an executive order by the President, Franklin D. Roosevelt, on February 19, 1942, which resulted in the removal and internment of 110,000 Japanese Americans from the West Coast to relocation camps scattered in various states.[17] Over two-thirds of them were American citizens.

The hardships, humiliation, economic losses, and severe loss of self-esteem caused by this action are described in many books. On July 30, 1944, the War Relocation Authority (WRA), an agency created to oversee the relocation camps, reported that not one instance of sabotage or espionage had occurred among citizens of Japanese ancestry; however, those who wished to return to the West Coast had to remain in the camps until 1945. Claims from this blatantly racist act are still in the process of settlement today.

A backward glance at this disgraceful event reveals that the motivation was more political than military. It is noteworthy that Hawaii, with a population of 150,000 people of Japanese ancestry, did not intern or detain any of these folks, even though Hawaii, because of its location, was more strategic and vulnerable to attack.

Unlike the Chinese, the Japanese in America had strong family lives, with the more favorable man-woman ratio and the practice of marriage by proxy (mail-order brides). In addition to the fact that the Japanese were quicker than were the Chinese to adopt Western dress, food, and other customs, some writers consider the Japanese family to have been the most significant factor in the social and economic upward mobility of Japanese Americans. The strong cultural values required for upward mobility were cultivated in a family setting. Since 1940, Japanese have led all other groups in the United States (including whites) in terms of amount of education, a result of family encouragement.[18] The high Japanese educational attainment is partially explained by the family values of conformity, aspiration, competitiveness, discipline, and self-control.[19] Japanese Americans have entered such professional fields as engineering, pharmacy, and other technical-scientific areas. Not only do they have higher incomes than any other nonwhite group in the United States, they are comparable to whites in occupational distribution and income.[20] However, as some writers point out, Japanese Americans are not often found in high-level executive positions in American-owned business and industry, though more and more Japanese are coming here to manage American-based, Japanese-owned firms.

Even though Japanese Americans continue to be victims of subtle prejudice and discrimination, many writers agree that their degree of cultural assimilation is high. While there is some conjecture over the degree of structural assimilation of Japanese Americans, one study showed that 50 percent of the males and females surveyed engage in outgroup dating and marriage.[21]

Rates of adult and juvenile crime, mental illness, and suicide of Japanese Americans are lower than for any other group. Much of this is attributed to the major institutions of Japanese culture and the resultant social controls.[22]

According to 1980 census figures, Japanese Americans are primarily urban dwellers, with approximately 70 percent living in the states of California (37.4 percent) and Hawaii (34.2 percent). States with significant Japanese American populations include Washington (3.8 percent), New York (3.5 percent), and Illinois (2.6 percent).

From 1970 to 1980, while the white population in the United States increased by 6 percent, the Japanese American population increased by 19 percent. This is considerably less of an increase than for other Asian groups in the United States.

Although Japanese Americans are economically successful, they remain politically powerless, except in Hawaii. Considered by many to be the most successful of American minority groups, they remain stereotyped as a visible ethnic minority group.

Background Readings: Japanese Americans[23]

Avaliable in paperback is *East to America: A History of the Japanese in the United States*, by Robert A. Wilson and Bill Hosokawa. It is recommended as "scholarly but lively" in volume 2 (Winter 1983) of *Focus on Asian Studies*.

Banks indicates that few comprehensive treatments of Japanese Americans exist, even though much has been written about the internment camps of World War II. Scholarly works recommended by Banks are *Japanese Americans: The Evolution of a Subculture*, by Harry H. L. Kitano; and *Japanese Americans: Oppression and Success*, by William Petersen. For additional information about Japanese Americans and other Asian Americans, Banks suggests the article "Asian Americans: A Success Story?" edited by Stanley Sue and Harry H. L. Kitano.

FILIPINO AMERICANS

The third major group of Asians to come to the West Coast was the Filipinos. Following the annexation of the Philippines in 1898 by the United States, Filipinos were placed in a "limbo" status in which they were "nationals" or "wards" of the United States, but not citizens (as were the Puerto Ricans). Early immigrants went to Hawaii as contract laborers to work the sugar plantations in 1908. Beginning in 1910, their numbers increased, so that by 1924, close to forty thousand lived on the islands, providing a source of cheap labor.[24] The Gentlemen's Agreement of 1908, mentioned earlier, substantially reduced Japanese immigration, and later, the Immigration Act of 1924 stopped the flow of cheap labor. Attempts to recruit cheap labor from Puerto Rico failed, but efforts to recruit workers from the Philippines were successful for large-scale farmers on the United States' West Coast.[25] Fishing and cannery industries of the Pacific Northwest eagerly sought Filipino laborers. During the "off-seasons," Filipino laborers worked as domestics in hotels, restaurants, and private homes.[26]

Immigration to the United States reached its peak in 1929, with 5,795 Filipinos entering California.[27] Early Filipino immigrants were mostly male, with over 80 percent under thirty years of age. Few women immigrated because female immigration violated tradition. Like other Asian sojourners, their intended stay in the United States was a temporary one, for their objective was to return to the Phillippines after becoming rich in America. This dream was unfulfilled for most, as they toiled in low-paying stoop-labor field work picking lettuce, asparagus, and other crops, or worked in canneries or domestic jobs as bellboys, waiters, cooks, busboys, janitors, houseboys, elevator operators, and hospital attendants.

Filipinos "inherited" the anti-Asian feelings in the West which had been expressed toward the previous Asian immigrants, the Chinese and Japanese. In addition to the anti-Asian attitudes, Filipino immigrants faced other problems. Many came with some command of the English language and with a literal interpretation of the creed that in the United States all men are created equal. This belief in equality with whites fostered many clashes in small towns in California and other states in the Northwest. The youth of the Filipino immigrants and the extreme shortage of Filipino women forced the males to seek the company of women of other races. Their courting of white women was the basis for a number of confrontations between Filipinos and whites. Some of these meetings ending in beatings, others in death. Several Western states prohibited marriage between Filipinos and Caucasians.[28]

Anti-Asian forces on the West Coast were joined by organized labor (the American Federation of Labor) and patriotic organizations (such as the Native Sons of the Golden West) in efforts to suppress the Filipinos. Cries from "unfair labor competition" to "unassimilable" were heard. Because they were not of alien status, their numbers could not be restricted. After failure by Rep. Richard Welch of California to pass an outright exclusion bill in Congress in 1928, a shift of tactics was utilized. The anti-Filipino forces heavily supported the Tydings-McDuffie Act of 1934, which granted the Philippines independence and at the same time limited Filipino immigration to fifty persons per year.[29] Still this did not satisfy the anti-Filipino forces, who also wanted Filipinos deported. Their efforts resulted in the passage of the Repatriation Act, which provided free transportation to any Filipino who wished to return to the Philippines. However, once they returned, they could not reenter the United States. Only about two thousand returned under these conditions.

By enlisting in the United States armed forces, a number of Filipinos gained United States citizenship upon the completion of military service, thus circumventing immigration quotas.[30] Many of these Filipino men emigrated, bringing their families to the United States.

During World War II, one-third of the Filipino men in the United States signed up to fight in the American military.[31] Many who stayed in the United States found jobs in defense industries, and some purchased farming lands in California from relocated Japanese Americans.

By 1946, following the close of World War II, the Filipino immigrantion quota was increased to one hundred.[32] Also, in the 1950s, an agreement between the United States and the Philippines resulted in the recruitment of thousands of Filipino men into the U.S. Navy as domestics and servants aboard the ships.[33] In 1952, a new quota system increased the number of allowable Filipino immigrants to two thousand per year. By the 1965 Immigration Act, this quota increased to above twenty thousand per year.

The characteristics of immigrants in the postwar years have changed drastically from those of the early immigrants. Newer arrivals consist of many skilled workers and professionals (teachers, doctors, and lawyers).[34] Some find employment in the United States consistent with their training and education; some do not. A continuation of discrimination, and differences in training and linguistics, force some of these professionals into laboring or service jobs. Some obtain professional jobs after additional American schooling. Before 1970, Filipino Americans were heavily concentrated in the lower strata of the population by indicators such as education, income, and job status. Since this time, however, the later census data show that Filipino Americans do not differ substantially from Japanese Americans and Chinese Americans.[35] It should be remembered, however, that averages conceal the wide range of extremes. A substantial number of Filipino Americans remain poor.

Filipino Americans are now the second largest group of people in the United States of Asian ancestry, yet they are lacking in political power as well as cultural identity. While European Americans study aspects of Chinese or Japanese culture, such as cooking, art, or the martial arts, Filipino culture remains largely unexplored.

Background Readings: Filipino Americans[36]

In *An Annotated List of Selected Resources for Promoting and Developing an Understanding of Asian Americans*, Peter Moy recommends resources which address the historical and contemporary struggle of Filipino Americans as well as literary works which reflect current expressions of Filipino American thought and feeling. Some of the recommendations are:

Canillo, Alex, et al., eds. *Pinoy: Know Yourself: An Introduction to the Filipino American Experience.*

Kim, Hyung-chan, and Cynthia C. Mejia. *The Filipinos in America, 1898–1974.*

Morales, Royal F. *Makibaka: The Filipino American Struggle.*

Munoz, Alfredo N. *The Filipinos in America.* Interviews with Filipino Americans reflect experiences of migrants, urban old-timers, and second-generation Filipino Americans.

Quinsaat, Jesse, ed. *Letters in Exile: An Introductory Reader on the History of Filipinos in America.*

Robles, Al, et., eds. *Liwang: Literary and Graphic Expressions.*

For information on the early immigration of Filipinos to Hawaii and the United States mainland, Banks recommends Bruno Lasker's *Filipino Immigration to Continental United States and Hawaii*, first published in 1931. A poignant book about Filipino life in the United States, according to Banks, is *America Is in the Heart*, by Carlos Bulosan. Other recommended titles by Miller in *A Handbook of American Minorities*, as well as by Banks, include *I Have Lived with the American People*, by Manuel Buaken and *Roots: An Asian American Reader*, edited by Amy Tachiki, Eddie Wong, and Franklin Odo.

KOREAN AMERICANS

In 1882, the United States became the first Western nation to sign a treaty with Korea formalizing friendship and trade relations. During this time, Korea, a peninsula bound by China on one side, Russia on another, and Japan on another, was under Chinese isolationist influence, although Japan had forced a treaty in 1876 that gave them a dominant role within Korea. The presence of the Japanese, combined with the influence of Christian missionaries and a famine, resulted in the immigration of 7,226 Koreans (637 of them women) between 1903 and 1905 as contract laborers. The first group went to Hawaii, with others going to the United States. Because of long hours and harsh conditions of plantation work in Hawaii, a thousand of this original group returned to Korea.[37] These laborers were needed in the Hawaiian sugar plantations to replace the dwindling labor supply which resulted from the Chinese exclusion by the 1882 legislation.

In 1907 there were approximately two thousand Korean laborers in San Francisco. Some had been recruited as railroad construction workers.[38] Others worked in agriculture and industry. During the 1900s various small communities on the West Coast became home to Korean immigrants. These include Dinuba and Reedley (California), in the San Joaquin Valley. Other settlements were started in Denver, Seattle, Salt Lake City, and Butte, Montana.

Because Korea had become a protectorate of Japan (similar to the protection status of the United States and the Philippines), Koreans in the United States had experienced a status similar to other Asians. That is, they were tolerated when they were small in numbers and filled needed laborers' positions. As they grew in numbers, they were perceived as a threat to white Americans, who often competed for the same jobs. They too experienced the racist reactions of white America to people of Asian ancestry. Pressures from various groups closed many jobs to Korean workers, leaving, for the most part, only the most menial ones.

As with the other Asian groups, picture brides helped to increase the numbers of Koreans in the United States between 1907 and 1924. There was a great age disparity between the picture brides and the older males, resulting in a number of second-generation Korean Americans spending part of their formative years with non-English-speaking widowed mothers with little formal education. The 1924 Immigration Act ended Japanese and Korean immigration, as well as that of the picture brides.[39]

From 1908 to 1924, the most visible group of Koreans in the United States were young and predominantly Christian. They led demonstrations around college campuses near Los Angeles and San Francisco, protesting the Japanese occupation of Korea.[40] Many studied Korean history and language in Korean organizations throughout California and Hawaii. By 1930, Japanese exploitation of Korea, which included using mineral resources, banning the Korean language in schools, requiring public use of Japanese language, and forcing Koreans to adopt Japanese names, intensified nationalistic feeling among Korean immigrants in the United States.

In 1940, a sizable cluster of Korean-owned businesses could be found in Los Angeles. These included vegetable stands, groceries, laundries, trucking companies, wholesalers, restaurants, drugstores, hat shops, an employment agency, and a rooming house.[41] By 1945, three thousand Koreans were living on the U.S. mainland, with sixty-five hundred in Hawaii. Many lived on the fringes of Chinatowns and Little Tokyos. Koreans were angered when mistaken for Japanese. They considered the Japanese to be oppressors in their home country and fierce competitors for jobs in America.

From 1951 until 1965, most of the immigration quotas for Korea were filled by students and war orphans, placed for adoption in the United States. Changes in the immigration laws in 1965 broadened immigration opportunities for both professionals and students by eliminating rigid quotas. Between 1947 and 1975, twenty-eight thousand Korean women, brides of United States servicemen, immigrated to the United States. They were not subject to quota restrictions.[42]

Before 1970, Koreans were listed in the U.S. census in the broad category of "other Asian." Between 1960 and 1970, sixty-two thousand Koreans were admitted to the United States on temporary visas, with many changing their status to permanent resident or immigrant as they completed their education here.[43]

A dramatic increase in the number of Korean immigrants between the years 1970 and 1975 occurred with 122,000 arrivals to the United States. The 1980 census recorded a Korean population of 354,000, which is five times the number recorded in 1970. As previously stated, they are the fourth largest Asian population in the United States.[44]

While Koreans have been in America for over seventy years, they are probably the least known of the Asian groups. In general, they are dispersed over the United States, except for Koreatown, a five-square-mile area in the Olympic region of Los Angeles, with approximately 150,000 Koreans.[45] Alumni clubs, trade associations, a vast variety of small businesses, and seventy-two Korean churches are among the organizations which service the established and recently arrived Koreans.

It is estimated that 72 percent of the residents of Koreatown held professional or managerial-level jobs before coming to the United States. Yet unemployment runs above the national average. Some of this is explained by the language difficulties and the variance in professional training requirements between countries.

Except for their visibility in Los Angeles and Honolulu, Koreans receive little attention in the popular media.[46] Some have attributed this to the lack of organizations (such as the Chinese Benevolent Associations or the Japanese-American Citizen League).

One of the best-known Korean Americans is Dr. Sammy Lee, who in 1952 became the first diver in Olympic history to win the first place in the high-diving competition twice in a row. He has been elected to the Diving Hall of Fame.[47]

Background Readings: Korean Americans[48]

In *An Annotated List of Selected Resources for Promoting and Developing an Understanding of Asian Americans*, Peter Moy indicates that limited amounts of good materials on the Korean American experience are available at present. He indicates that additional historical and literary materials are being written. Among the materials recommended by Moy are the following:

Kim, Hyung-Chan, and Wayne Patterson, eds. and comp. *The Koreans in America, 1882–1974. A Chronology and Fact Book.*

Kim, Warren Y. *Koreans in America.* Moy considers this an indispensable book about Korean experiences in the United States from 1902 to 1948. Information on migration, religious, and educational and cultural activities is presented, in addition to the Korean political activities that predominate in this work. Moy says the interesting readings provide insight into the unique experiences which set Korean Americans apart from other Asian American groups.

Koh, Kwang Lim, and Hesung C. Koh, eds. *Koreans and Korean Americans in the United States. Their Problems and Perspectives. A Summary of Three Conference Proceedings, 1971–1973.*

Sunoo, Brenda Paik, ed. *Korean American Writings: Selected Material from* INSIGHT, *Korean American Bimonthly.* Three sections comprise this work: Community, Patriotic Movement, and Poetry. Themes of the material include identity, history, immigration, politics, and poetry from three generations of Korean Americans.

Recent publications related to Korean Americans include:

Baker, Houston A., Jr., ed. *Three American Literatures: Essays in Chicano, Native American and Asian American Literature.*

Kim, Elaine H. *Asian American Literature: An Introduction to the Writings and Their Social Context.*

Kim, Illsoo. *New Urban Immigrants: The Korean Community in New York.*

Nakanishi, Don T., and Marsha Hirano-Nakanishi, eds. *The Education of Asian and Pacific Americans: Historical Perspectives and Prescriptions for the Future.*

Thernstrom, Stephan, Ann Orlav, and Oscar Handlin, eds. *Harvard Encyclopedia of American Ethnic Groups.*

VIETNAMESE AMERICANS

As the war in Vietnam ended in the spring of 1975, the United States evacuated 140,000 refugees who feared for their safety. Many of the refugees, like the early Cuban immigrants, left because of political, not economic, reasons. Most of these refugees were women and children, but others were doctors, lawyers, storeowners, and professional people. Nearly half spoke English, and many were well educated and had marketable skills.[49]

Of the 140,000, some went to France or Canada to live, some decided to return to Vietnam, and 127,000 were placed in seven relocation centers in the United States to wait for American sponsors. Also included were four thousand Cambodians. Initial American public opinion on such governmental action was negative. Economic conditions were not favorable, and some saw the refugees as an economic threat. Others had negative feelings concerning the war in Vietnam and projected these feelings on the refugees. With still others, racial opposition to Asian immigrants was the reason for objection.

Within seven months, through the generous support of church groups, all refugees found sponsors. In fact, there were more potential sponsors than refugees at the end of the seven months. No other refugee group of such a large size has been resettled in the United States in such a short time period.

Between April 1975 and July 1979, 220,000 Indo-Chinese refugees were granted permanent residence in the United States. By July 1979, the growing number of Vietnamese "boat people" seeking refuge prompted President Carter to double the United States quota to fourteen thousand refugees a month.

The Vietnamese refugees have been scattered all over the country, with some being sent to Alaska. The largest concentrations are in California, Texas, Pennsylvania, Florida, and Washington. Other large concentrations are in New Orleans, Arlington (Virginia), the Washington, D.C., area and Los Angeles.[50] Of the 261,714 Vietnamese counted in the 1980 census, 119,986 live in western states, with California accounting for 89,587 of this number. Southern states have over 80,000 Vietnamese, the north central states show a count of over 36,000, and the northeastern states have the least, numbering almost 25,000.

Life has not been easy for the Vietnamese in the United States. Even with the first wave (1975) of immigrants, who were well educated and had held professional or management positions, many were forced to work at jobs substantially below their previous level, because of language and cultural barriers, as well as economic conditions in the United States.[51] The second wave (1979), who escaped by boat were lacking education and training, so that their occupational opportunities have been limited in this country. Some advantages to the later arrivals were that Vietnamese had, by this time, formed self-help organizations for those with limited communication skills in English. Others of the late arrivals had relatives already living in the United States. Less help was given to the 1979 refugees by the government for resettlement. Refugees who received help with their airfare to the United States in 1979 signed an agreement to repay part of this expense.[52]

All immigrants face adjustment problems as old-and new-world values and cultures clash, but Vietnamese refugees, like many other Indo-Chinese immigrants, faced additional burdens. Unique psychological, social, and economic adjustments had to be made. The traumatic effects of war and the disjointing of families with very close ties posed psychological problems. Rapid transition to a vastly different cultural surrounding with changed language, values, status, and lifestyles, demands tremendous social adaptation. Some of the men lost status because they were unable to practice their profession and had to take jobs as factory workers, busboys, or waiters. This situation was not only one of economic consequence, but one which threatened the father's position as head of the household, especially if his wife worked outside of the home for the first time.

Children, as well as adults, faced adjustments in the new country. In traditional Vietnamese culture, children are expected to respect older persons and display respect by being quiet, polite, modest, and humble. This is in sharp contrast to the average middle-class child, who may be characterized as assertive, independent, and verbal. Resolving these differences in behavioral tolerances poses real problems for Vietnamese children in school and at home.

Another adjustment for children is in the area of schooling. Vietnamese children are taught to respect the authority of the teacher, which means not to challenge that authority nor to question a teacher. Teachers in Vietnam use the lecture method of teaching. The discovery approach to learning, increasingly used in American schools, poses problems for Vietnamese children.

Practicing the concept of "phuc duc" and a strong belief in astrology affects the lives of many Vietnamese. The concept of "phuc duc" is that good fortune is related to one's meritorious or self-sacrificing actions. This is secured primarily by a woman for her family and affects the lives of others into the fifth generation. Personal sacrifice or improper conduct can increase or diminish the amount of "phuc duc."[53]

At the time of birth, a Vietnamese astrologer predicts the future events of the newborn, as well as the personality. This form of self-fulfilling prophecy largely determines the child's rearing practices, as well as the actions of the child. This deterministic approach to life has greatly influenced the adaptation of the Vietnamese in America.

A study done on the first wave of Vietnamese immigrants showed that those with a higher level of education, prior travel experience abroad, and a higher degree of Americanization prior to emigration achieved higher levels of acculturation. While reaction to these refugees has been mixed, they have been welcomed in most communities. More of them are changing from refugee status to that of immigrants and to full-fledged American citizens. The tenacity they have displayed in overcoming so many obstacles has been admired by many.

A deep respect for learning is a long-held value of Vietnamese people. With students working hard, having a love for booklearning, and showing respect for the teacher, it is reasonable to expect that a fair number of Vietnamese refugee children will go on to university studies.

Background Readings: Vietnamese Americans[54]

Buttinger, Joseph. *The Dragon Defiant: A Short History of Vietnam.*
Hall, D.C. *A History of South-East Asia.*
Nguyên Du. *The Tale of Kiêu: A Bilingual Edition of Tryên Kiêu.*
Osborne, Milton. *Southeast Asia: An Introductory History.*
"Vietnam: A Teacher's Guide."
Vuong G. Thuy. *Getting to Know the Vietnamese and Their Culture.*
Whitmore, John K., ed. *An Introduction to Indo-Chinese History, Culture, Language and Life.*

LAOTIAN AMERICANS

The fall of Indo-China in 1975 included Laos, Cambodia (Kampuchea), and Vietnam. Those refugees who were in the early (1975) group had some acquaintance with Western culture and were the most educated. As in Vietnam, because of the long presence and the rule of the French, certain institutions, such as primary schools and courts, were patterned after French models.

Thousands of refugees from Laos who have been resettled in the United States include Tai, Hmong, ethnic Laotians, and a small number of Mien and Lao Theung. Ethnic Laotians comprise the largest group in Laos and have close cultural and linguistic ties with people of northern Thailand.[55] The dialect of the Tai people is similar to that of speakers of Laotian, so they can usually understand each other. Hmong and Mien people are recent immigrants from southern China and retain the influences of Chinese culture. They are mountain people who subsist on agriculture and livestock raising. Many Hmong and Mien speak Laotian.

Lao Theung are the upland Laotians, who are descendants of earlier ethnic groups that arrived before the Tai.

Laotians, then, are not a singular but a complex group of diverse ethnic subgroups encompassing, varied languages and lifestyles. Many of the Laotians adhere to the dominant religion, Therevada Buddhism.[56] As Buddhists, they practice "king-chai," which includes respecting others, maintaining modesty, and avoiding confrontation.

Transition from a predominantly village life based on customs and beliefs of long standing to the detached, urban American society has not been without pain. Like other Asian immigrants, change to the new life has been easier for the children and more difficult for the adults. A 1981 report of the U.S. Office of Refugee Resettlement gives the count of 141,000 people from Laos living in the United States. At that time, they represented 5 percent of all Asian Americans in the United States.

Background Readings: Laotian Americans[58]

Department of the Army. *Area Handbook for. Laos.*
Garrett, Wilbur E. "No Place to Run: The Hmong of Laos."
Lebar, Frank, and Adrienne Suddar. *Laos: Its People, Its Society, Its Culture.*
Lutheran Immigration Services. *The Hmong: Their History and Culture.*
Outsama, Kao. *Laotian Themes.* (Information about customs, education, and learning styles in Laos.)
Perazic, Elizabeth. "Little Laos, Next Door to Red China."
Tambiah, S. J. *Buddhism and the Spirit Cults in Northeast Thailand.*

KAMPUCHEAN AMERICANS

Kampuchea (formerly known as Cambodia), which is bordered by Thailand, Laos, Vietnam, and the Gulf of Siam, is another Indo-Chinese country which was overthrown by Communists in 1975, sending refugees to the United States as well as to other countries. During the Communist take-over, under Pol Pot, cities were evacuated and hundreds of thousand Kampucheans died or were killed.[59] It is estimated that one-fourth or more of Kampuchea's population died at the hands of Pol Pot and the Khmer Rouge government. An Asian holocaust of starvation and mass extermination, it was referred to by the wire services in 1978 as the "Auschwitz of Asia."[60]

Nearly 90 percent of the people are descendants of the Khmer, who share many physical and cultural traits with the Thais and the Burmese. Cultural minorities include Vietnamese, who work in farming and industry; Chinese, who are fish and rice merchants; and the Chams, Islamic weavers and traders of Indonesian stock. Many Kampucheans who lived in urban areas speak French and Khmer, since French was used in education and government prior to 1975.[61]

Problems of Kampuchean refugees in the United States have been similar to those of other refugees from Indochina; however, the Kampucheans have experienced much more family disintegration due to the many wars fought in their land, the horrible atrocities, and the resultant short supply of food and services which decimated many.[62] Pol Pot, whose regime was backed by the Chinese Communists, was forced to flee in the mountains in 1978 by the invading North Vietnamese, who were backed by the Soviet Union. The continued guerrilla attack by Pol Pot and the occupation of the land by North Vietnam forces sent more refugees out of the country. In 1979, as many as 400,000 refugees were in camps in Thailand. In 1980, it was estimated that Kampuchea's population of eight million had been reduced to four or five million.[63]

Old memories and deep-rooted fear plague many Kampuchean Americans. Some feel guilty for surviving. Like some of the American veterans of the Vietnam War, they suffer from a mental health condition which has been identified as "post-traumatic stress disorder."[64] Since their numbers are not as great as other Americans of Asian ancestry, there are not as many Kampuchean neighborhoods in the United States. Yet there are several Kampuchean (Cambodian) organizations in this country which attempt to help others. Ethnic familiarity and the sharing of common beliefs and values have, throughout the history of the United States, served as a buffer between the ethnic individual and the larger society.

Many Kampuchean refugees have been able to utilize their job skills and education in order to find employment here.[65] By pooling resources into "family" groups, they are able to buy homes and automobiles and sponsor other arrivals.

A large number of single-parent families headed by a woman have been created by family dislocation among Kampuchean refugees. This presents special problems for these women. In Kampuchea, a strict code of conduct for females was followed; young girls were not allowed to go out at night or to talk casually with young men. Conflicts arise when teenagers express the same desire for freedom in this area as they see in their American counterparts.

In 1981, the U.S. Office of Refugee Resettlement estimated the number of Kampuchean refugees in this country to be 102,000. This represents three percent of all Asian Americans.[66] Because of the decreased admission of Vietnamese refugees and the steady increase of Kampuchean refugees to the United States, the Indo-Chinese American makeup is gradually changing.

Background Readings: Kampuchean Americans[67]

Allman, T. D. "Cambodia: Nightmare Journey to a Doubtful Dawn."
Chandler, Daivd P. *A History of Cambodia.*
Coedès, G. *The Making of Southeast Asia.*
Garrett, Wilbur E. "The Temples of Angkor: Will They Survive?"
Vek, Huong Tiang. *Ordeal in Cambodia: One Family's Escape from the Khmer Rouge.*
White, Peter T. "Kampuchea Awakens from a Nightmare."

PART 3
INTRODUCTION

Biased material is a continuing problem. The content—both words and pictures—in materials reflects prejudice and discrimination as it exists within society. As seen in the brief descriptions of various cultural groups in chapters 3 and 4, many members of Hispanic and Asian-Pacific cultural minorities in the United States have had to endure practices resulting from discrimination in their encounters with persons of mainstream and other cultures.

There is a pressing need to provide for all American children and youth educational programs and materials that will help them learn to value the cultural pluralism of our society—their own cultural heritages as well as that of others.

For new immigrants, materials are needed to provide information associated with adjustments to the new country. Language, customs, mores, laws, and vocations are among the areas of informational needs.

Chapter 5 describes some approaches to examining materials and explores criteria typically used in preparing librarians and teachers to select and use books and other media. This report is an investigation into selection guidelines and related inservice practices reported by public librarians and school library media supervisors as they provide services for Hispanic and Asian-Pacific children and youth in 1984.

Chapter 6 describes additional materials from which selection guidelines can be derived and selected agencies which can facilitate the development of a personal network of contacts to assist in the selection process. The agencies are potential resources for information, bibliographies, curricular materials and guides, professional materials, or resource persons.

Chapter 5
Selection of Culturally Relevant Materials: Guidelines and Related Issues

CRITERIA: A STEP IN THE SELECTION PROCESS

Identification of criteria is one of several steps needed to develop a collection of materials to serve a potential group of users. Phyllis J. Van Orden identifies ten steps in a process she describes as the "collection program."[1]

The ten steps require an action-oriented librarian to: (1) review knowledge of the existing collection or determine the need to create a new collection; (2) become acquainted with the community; (3) assess needs of school or community programs and users; (4) develop a collection development plan by establishing policies and procedures in relation to short-and long-term library goals; (5) create specific policies and procedures as the basis for implementing the selection process; (6) identify criteria to provide the basis for evaluation of materials; (7) plan the step-by-step procedures of the selection process, which include: (a) assessing others' contributions to decisions, (b) determining and obtaining selection tools needed, and (c) arranging for personal examination of materials; (8) establish guidelines and procedures to obtain the materials and equipment; (9) plan and establish procedures for keeping the materials and equipment of the collection in good repair; and (10) plan a comprehensive continuous evaluation process which can provide guidance when needed for steps one through nine.

The ten-step process is that specified by Van Orden in *The Collection Program in Elementary and Middle Schools: Concepts, Practices and Information Sources.* The interpretations of this process are those of the authors who find them to be comprehensive and adaptable to librarians who provide leadership for the development of collections to serve children and young adults in public libraries as well as in school libraries.

The definition and explanations by Van Orden for the term "criteria" are useful for persons who develop collections of material to serve the needs of children and youth. Van Orden[2] says, "Criteria, the standards by which items will be evaluated, are a major part of the selection policy. Criteria that assess the item itself and its relation to the collection development policy must be established. Generally accepted criteria include: literary quality, currency, accuracy of information, appeal and value to children, application within the curriculum, and quality and format of presentation. Criteria need to be established for specific formats or for *materials to be used by specific types of users*" (italics are the authors', since this bears directly on our subject).[2]

Helen Huus[3] takes a wholistic approach to the evaluation of children's books as literature.[3] She describes a process of multiple evaluations in which a book is screened by the author, editor, and publisher; the purchaser; and ultimately the user. Huus examines the elements of quality usually considered in evaluating children's materials. Three are identified as format, content and style.

Format and its appropriateness, with that of the illustrations' color, technique, and medium, to the content of a book is discussed, with works of author-illustrator Marcia Brown used as examples. Overall quality of bookmaking is reviewed also for its contributions to the format.

For the second element, content, Huus points out the necessity for examining theme, setting, plot, characters, and style. Theme, according to Huus, involves the overarching idea: the answer to "What is the book about?" However, the qualities of the theme may merit examination using the criteria of "good, true, and beautiful." Goodness is equated with values portrayed, trueness is related to the attributes of accuracy and realness, and beauty is defined by the appraiser. Setting, says Huus, should be evaluated for accuracy and clarity in descriptions of the locale and the era so that they are comprehensible to the reader. Plot provides the framework for the events of the book. Plot is equated with the story, the elements of conflict, and their subsequent resolution. Characters, when convincing, are true to real-life or fanciful counterparts. Huus claims that clues to good depiction of characters are found by examining "what characters say and think and do, what others say about them, and how they are depicted in the illustrations."

Style involves the use of words and sentences and the manner in which an author conveys ideas. Criteria for factual accounts are different from those for imaginative works.

Grace W. Ruth provides advice about selection criteria in her 1983 article entitled "Selecting Children's Books to Meet Multicultural Needs." Ruth was the book evaluation and administrative assistant at the Office of Children's Services in the San Francisco Public Library at the time she wrote this article. Ruth advocates that materials about minority cultures; (1) meet the criteria for good literature; (2) present minorities in a positive manner—factual but nonjudgmental—in text and illustrations; and (3) not perpetuate prejudices and stereotypes in text and illustrations.[4] "By meeting the needs of new immigrant and minority children, libraries provide enrichment not only for those particular children, but for all those with whom they share a community. Reflecting social pluralism and responding to change are challenges that require librarians to continually reexamine their goals and collections." Ruth reaffirms the importance of assessing community needs and of finding materials to meet the needs identified.

POTENTIAL EFFECTS OF MATERIALS ON CHILDREN AND YOUTH

The *effect* of materials on children and youth must be a concern of those involved in the selection of ethnic materials. James Anderson advocates the development of comprehensive criteria for evaluating this effect. According to him, objectionable or misrepresentative information concerning a specific ethnic group may be "deliberate or unintentional, cognitive or affective, direct or implied, or may result from the omission of certain pertinent information."[5]

Specific and accurate information are important criteria for nonfiction. Textbooks as well as library materials are subject to misrepresentations and inaccuracies. J. D. McAulay describes criteria used by fourteen graduate students in education from Thailand, Vietnam, Laos, and Cambodia to examine and evaluate seven social studies textbooks which were, in 1978, being used in a tenth-grade unit on Southeast Asia in five randomly selected Pennsylvania high schools.

The three criteria were: (1) "Are the mores and customs of the people of Southeast Asia pictured realistically?"; (2) "Is the history of this political region given with some accuracy?"; (3) "Is the topography presented with some geographic accuracy?"[6]

The evaluators found numerous nonrealistc portrayals of Southeast Asian people. The findings from their examination of the textbooks showed:

1. Failure to indicate that people of Southeast Asia (Thailand, Burma, Laos, and Vietnam) all came originally from China and are Mongoloid.
2. Ascribing to these people the habit of chewing betel nut when this had never been observed.
3. Failure to indicate the piety associated with giving to yellow-robed Buddhist monks or the fact that, for males, becoming monks for a period of time is a required part of their education.
4. Indication that a type of sarong is a common article of feminine clothing, but failure to state that a different style and name for it exists in each country.
5. Untrue statement that small families composed of parents and children are common to Southeast Asian countries. Actually, married sons and daughters live with parents and other relatives, operating as a close-knit group within agricultural societies.
6. Erroneous facts about the percentages of populations belonging to given religions.
7. Attribution of political influence to religious groups in a country, such as Thailand, where religion is completely separated from politics.
8. Indication of underpopulation in a country where the contrary is true.
9. Attribution of loyalty of a country's residents to their land of origin when actually second-generation onward are considered citizens (again, the error concerned Thailand).
10. Distribution of more space to Indonesia and the Philippines than to mainland countries.
11. Statements of erroneous information concerning the Emerald Buddha, the most worshiped object of Thailand, and failure to give the Laotian name, Phra Bang, for this Buddha.
12. Implication that India and China expanded to exert influence and control of trade when the first purpose had been to teach Buddhism.

13. Omissions of names of countries in which important rivers exist.
14. Statement that Rangoon is a port but failure to mention that it is a capital.
15. Omission of the fact that oil is found in abundance in West Burma.
16. Inclusion of territories as portions of Southeast Asia which are not known to be so by the residents of the area.
17. Inferior and insufficient illustrations to give readers an overall impression of living in Southeast Asia.
18. Inadequate maps which lack detailed information.
19. Too much emphasis on the role which Southeast Asian nations are playing in current affairs.
21. Principal concerns in the textbooks should be: (a) culture; (b) religions; (c) patterns of living; and (d) social values.
22. More space should be given to occupations, because they reflect economic and social conditions as well as the problems of the nations.
23. Maps recommended to be included within the content were: (a) an overall map to show the relationship of Southeast Asia to the entire continent of Asia; (b) a map to illustrate the topography; and (c) a map to show the political divisions.
24. Photographs and illustrations should provide details and supportive information to the content.[7]

While it is true that some of the above points (criticisms) are matters of opinion, clearly, the need for truthfulness, accuracy, and specificity of information characterize many of the objections indicated concerning the social-studies textbooks. It seems evident that review of materials by persons with an accurate knowledge of facts concerning cultural, historical, and geographical conditions of a country should take place before they are published rather than afterward.

SELECTION CRITERIA RELATED TO CULTURES IN CHILDREN'S LITERATURE

In the 1979 edition of *Children's Literature in the Elementary School*, Charlotte S. Huck[8] presents "Guidelines for Evaluating Children's Literature," which consists of questions which an evaluator can use to examine a book in terms of plot, setting, theme, characterization, style, and formal and other considerations.[8] Under the heading "Characterization," one of the questions posed is, "Does the author avoid stereotyping?"

Like Anderson and the Southeast Asian graduate students, Huck explains that stereotypes may involve the *omission* of significant facts. Huck says a blatant form of stereotyping, that of making sweeping generalizations, may be seen in books about other lands. She says children can be taught to watch for this, and question it. She asserts that diversity can be shown either by showing varieties of lifestyles or by limiting the scope of a particular book, and points out that appropriate generalizations are those which are supported by facts.

Margaret R. Marshall indicates other ways to identify racism in her 1982 edition of *An Introduction to the World of Children's Books*. Marshall[9] says, "Racism can be identified in books in which white people have power and make decisions regardless of the black or ethnic group in the story; where minority peoples are always presented as a 'problem'; where the effect on the child reader's self-image or self-esteem is likely to be damaging."[9]

Zena Sutherland, Dianne L. Monson, and May Hill Arbuthnot remind their readers in the 1981 edition of *Children and Books* that evaluation of children's books should "be neither a casual, uncritical approach nor a rigid adherence to the standards for adult literature."[10] In their section concerning areas and issues related to children and books, there is a selection entitled "Internationalism in Children's Literature," by Anne Pellowski, written when she was director-librarian of the Information Center on Children's Cultures, United Nations Children's Fund (UNICEF), in New York City.[11]

Pellowski identifies three important aspects of internationalism related to children's literature: (1) development of materials in areas of the world where children have had few opportunities to experience them in libraries and cultural centers; (2) exchange of materials for children in original or translated forms; and (3) the way different cultures are depicted in children's materials of a given country. Pellowski points out that visitors from small, developing countries are sometimes surprised to find more materials about their cultures in the English language than can be found in their own vernaculars. The materials in English are usually produced by North American or European writers and illustrators who have spent time in the areas.

Pellowski indicates questions which can be used to establish the validity of fictional and folkloric materials. She advocates examination of: (1) introductory material, to ascertain if the material has been created by a participant of the culture or an observer of it; (2) the total work, to see if elements which are morally or socially unacceptable within the United States have been removed or if, indeed, they are so intrinsic to values of the other society that they have been retained; (3) the material, to see if it is historical and, if so, is clearly shown to be so; and (4) the material, to see if it is folkloric and, if so, clearly indicates sources.

Pellowski poses other questions related to illustrations, photographs, and films. The questions concern:

1. Obvious stereotyping—pigtails for Chinese children, no clothes on African children, and barefoot boys on burros for Mexican children.
2. Facial characteristics of a given race depicted as the same, although there are infinite varieties within all racial groups.
3. Possible exaggerations about the comparative wealth or poverty of a nation or people.
4. Possible overemphasis on rural life, with little attention given to urban life.
5. Unusually different customs shown for shock value rather than explained as a part of the culture being investigated.

Pellowski suggests questions for factual materials as well. These questions relate to the examination of:

1. The copyright date for any limits on usability (datedness).
2. The copyright date, which (should be), when recent, a reflection of the latest changes related to geographical and political facts.
3. The point of view—to learn if the insider or the outsider, or both, is represented.
4. The sources—to find out what kind are given.

Pellowski is aware that each evaluator may not possess in-depth knowledge of a distant region or culture; however, she says a condescending tone or an oversimplified explanation of a complex matter may be signals that bias exists. She states it is better not to introduce children to another culture unless it can be done with sensitivity and care. Although children need to see the differences as well as the similarities of events, Pellowski warns that "different" should not be equated by children with "inferior."

Picture books in other languages enhance the self-image of young children who know a language other than the one primarily used by their peer group. Older children benefit from materials which contain concepts of nationality, country, region, and continent in addition to social and cultural values.

The importance of examining the cultural messages of materials to be selected for use with children and young people is emphasized by Donna E. Norton in her 1983 textbook *Through the Eyes of a Child.* Norton discusses "nonstereotypes" in a chapter on "Selecting Literature for Children," and provides another chapter entitled "Multiethnic Literature." She urges that children be provided with literature that presents authentic pictures of peoples, their cultures, and their historical contributions. Norton affirms not only the importance of enhancing the self-concepts of children from the given cultures studied, but also that of allowing all children to understand that each ethnic group, as well as their own, has persons with needs, feelings, and emotions similar to theirs. Reading the poetry, philosophy, history, traditional folk literature, geography, and biographies of other cultures can lead children to gain understanding of their own and other ethnic groups.

Norton says discussion and other reinforcing activities must follow the reading of positive multiethnic literature; this interaction between children and adults is necessary "if attitudes and self-concepts are to change." Norton points out that few books exist in the United States about Hispanic or Asian American people, and relays the concern of Mauricio Charpenel, consultant to the Mexican Ministry of Education, that the beautiful Latin American poetry which is available is not being shared with Mexican American children in the United States.

Norton's list of questions to use for evaluating Hispanic literature alerts the evaluator to avoid books which imply "that poverty is a natural condition of all Hispanics" or that problems are solved by the intervention of Anglo-Americans or by learning to speak English. In addition, evaluators are advised to determine if: (1) the cultural information is accurate; (2) the culture depicted is treated with respect; and (3) the illustrations show individuals rather than stereotypes. Language should not include derogatory terms or descriptions. Any dialects used should be normal parts of stories and not suggestive of stereotypes. Each book should be inspected for literary merit as well as correct spellings and uses of Spanish words.[12]

Norton cites the criteria developed by the Council on Interracial Books for Children for evaluating Asian American literature. The council advocates that a book reflect the realities of life as experienced by Asian American people. Overemphasis on portrayal of only one social or economic class and exaggerations about customs and festivals should be avoided. Stereotypical characterization should be avoided; a realistic range of human emotions should be portrayed (avoidance of docility); and stereotypes relative to occupations (avoiding portrayal of all Asian American persons as working in laundries or restaurants) should be watched for. There should be no historical distortions and omissions. Problems should not be resolved by benevolent white persons or by outstanding minority persons. Women should be portrayed in various roles, not always as subservient persons. Illustrations should show racial diversity and avoid depicting Asian American persons as looking alike. In addition, clothing and settings should be appropriately depicted.

Examination of the three textbooks by Huck; Sutherland, Monson, and Arbuthnot; and Norton leads to the conclusion that increasing emphasis is being placed upon the importance of materials which possess cultural validity. The textbooks with the most recent copyright dates provide the most discussion of these topics (see previous discussions of information presented in *Children and Books* and *Through the Eyes of a Child*). Marshall's discussion of the recent emphasis on translations and on the development of national research centers concerning children's books indicates that the need for culturally valid materials is felt worldwide.

CULTURAL FAIRNESS AND MATERIALS

A frequently reprinted list of selection criteria to use with materials for children is "Ten Quick Ways to Analyze Children's Books for Sexism and Racism," in *Guidelines for Selecting Bias-Free Textbooks and Storybooks*.[13] Users of the guidelines are invited to utilize them as a starting point for evaluating children's books. Explanations and examples are given in each of the ten areas of concern. The user of "Ten Quick Ways"[13] is advised to check: (1) illustrations, for stereotypes, tokenism, and the active and passive roles of the characters; (2) storyline, for indications of how success is defined, how problems are resolved, and what are the roles of women; (3) lifestyles, for implied negative values, residences of minority persons, and inaccuracies or inappropriateness in treatment of other cultures; (4) relationships between individuals, to ascertain who makes decisions and how relationships within families are shown; (5) heroes, for representation of the interests of the hero's people; (6) the effects on a child's self-image of connotations associated with the colors white and black, sex, and arbitrary definitions of beauty; (7) the author's and / or illustrator's qualifications as creators of the materials being examined; (8) the author's perspective; (9) words which are offensive; and (10) the copyright date as it might reflect an era when many materials about minorities were hastily produced, as in the 1960s. The council recommends that a child be shown how to detect racism and sexism in materials.

These brief indications of some of the concerns shown in the "Ten Quick Ways" are not exhaustive. Although this list of selection criteria is frequently reprinted in other publications, use of the additional information provided in the publication itself is helpful. It shows the extent to which bias has been identified in materials which are made available for the use of children and young people. The *Guidelines* contains reports which have resulted from several research studies conducted by the Council on Interracial Books for Children, as well as excerpts of criteria from other publications.

Although a number of evaluative procedures for materials have been suggested up to this point, it may be useful to examine actual current practices. To ascertain current practices and concern, selected findings of a recent survey are reported.

SURVEY OF PUBLIC AND SCHOOL LIBRARIES

A survey was made by the authors to seek information related to the topics of this book. In January 1984, letters were forwarded to the directors of public libraries and to the school library media supervisors of the fifty largest cities in the United States, those identified in the 1980 census as having the greatest amounts of population.

Responses were received from twenty public libraries and eight school districts. Thus, the total survey response was 28 percent.

The letter included the following requests, with a copy of the book's working outline:

Your assistance and guidance are needed.
(1) If you have a copy of selection criteria used to build collections of materials for and about children and young people who are either Spanish-speaking or of East Asian heritages,

e.g., Chinese, Japanese, Korean, Filipino, Kampuchean, Vietnamese or Laotian, will you forward a copy for use in preparation of the publication?

(2) If you have recommended inservice activities which you have used with your professional and / or nonprofessional personnel, will you please send a copy of these also?

(3) Any other additional information which would be useful for this project, such as names and addresses of other individuals or agencies, will be appreciated.[14]

Responses

The twenty public librarians' responses were separated into three geographical areas representative of the west coast, the central, and the east coast regions. They are listed as they might appear on a map from north to south within each region.

Regional Groups: Public Librarians

Western[15]
1. Seattle Public Library
2. Library Association of Portland
3. San Francisco Public Library
4. County of Los Angeles Public Library
5. Albuquerque Public Library
6. County of San Diego, County Library

Central[16]
7. Milwaukee Public Library
8. Chicago Public Library
9. Detroit Public Library
10. Indianapolis–Marion County
11. The Public Library of Cincinnati and Hamilton County
12. Louisville Free Public Library
13. Tulsa City-County Library System

Eastern[17]
14. Buffalo and Erie County Public Library
15. The New York Public Library
16. Newark Public Library
17. Free Library of Philadelphia
18. District of Columbia Public Library

19. Atlanta-Fulton Public Library
20. Miami-Dade Public Library System

The School Library Media Supervisors' responses were tallied separately:

National Group:[18] *School District Libraries*
21. Seattle Public Schools
22. Portland Public Schools
23. Los Angeles Unified School District
24. Albuquerque Public Schools
25. Oakwood Junior-Senior High School, Dayton, Ohio
26. Indianapolis Public Schools
27. El Paso Independent School District
28. Buffalo Public Schools

Brief summaries of the information gathered from each responding group follow. The roles of the respondents are reported, since roles influence the perceptions about information reported.

Examples of the information provided from the four groups are given after each summary. In some cases, additional details or the wording of the original response may be of interest.

Summary of Findings — Public Libraries, Western Region

1. Respondents to the requests for information about selection criteria, inservice, and other matters for the six public libraries included: two directors; three coordinators of children's services; one coordinator of young adult services; one children's book evaluator; one head, Main Library; one Outreach Services coordinator.
2. Community needs are emphasized as an important basis for the selection of materials. Five of the six libraries indicated that the publications of the Council on Interracial Books for Children are valued for providing guidance concerning the selection of children's materials. Two libraries indicated the usefulness of *Reading Ladders for Human Relations*, edited by Eileen Tway.[19] Specific titles, agencies, and individuals were cited as sources of additional information about: (1) sensitivity to other peoples and cultures; (2) foreign language publications; (3) vendors of materials from other countries; and (4) specialized bibliographies. Contributions of bicultural and bilingual personnel are valued for selection and programming. Involvement of members of the ethnic groups being addressed is

advocated. A need was cited for lists of sources for purchase of bilingual material and material in non-English languages.

3. Inservice is carried out in a variety of ways: training sessions, inservice meetings in the library, professional reading, professional association workshops, university courses, and programs provided by the library. One response indicated that library-sponsored inservice sessions were attended by paraprofessional as well as professional staff members.

4. The library system which reported programming activities showed that individuals from community groups were featured as presenters and were among the organizing persons. The programs served some of the inservice needs of library staff.

EXCERPTS—WESTERN REGION: PUBLIC LIBRARIES

Respondent role: Coordinator, Young Adult Services (response no. 1).

Inservice—"I believe that we wish to be sensitive to other people and cultures, but may need information and training to achieve that goal." *Reading Ladders for Human Relations* is recommended as a source of literature to extend sensitivity.

Other advice included consulting articles by Prof. Spencer Shaw, School of Library and Information Science, University of Washington; the Ethnic Materials Information Exchange Round Table, American Library Association; and the Tools for Consciousness-Raising Task Force, Bradford Chambers, Coordinator, Council on Interracial Books for Children.

* * *

Respondent role: Acting Assistant Coordinator, Children's Services (response no. 3).

Selection guidelines—Copies of two articles by Grace W. Ruth were forwarded. The articles are: "Notes for Talk at the U.S. Friends of IBBY Meeting, September 1, 1983," *Friends of IBBY Newsletter* 8 (Summer-Fall 1983): 3-5; and "Selecting Children's Books to Meet Multicultural Needs," *Catholic Library World* 55 (November 1983): 169-73.

Selection criteria are discussed on pages 169-71 of the latter article. Ruth says, "It is important to identify community needs." Community contacts with many agencies and organizations are very important. The second important criterion, states Ruth, is "to find quality books to meet your community needs." Selection standards are: (1) "Books about minority cultures meet the criteria for all good literature;" (2) books present "minorities in a positive manner in both illustration and text;" and (3) books not perpetuating "prejudices and stereotypes either in text or illustration." The *Bulletin* of the Council on Interracial Books for Children (CIBC) and the pamphlet "10 Quick Ways to Analyze Books for Racism and Sexism," issued by the CIBC were cited.

Ruth advocates including books which "show the contributions of minorities to the history and growth" of the United States, as well as books which "show minorities as an integral part of our society today." Classics and popular contemporary stories in translation can be included. Outstanding titles in translation include those which receive the yearly Mildred E. Batchelder Award from the Association for Library Service to Children of the American Library Association.

Among the specialized bibliographies recommended are: *Reading Ladders for Human Relations*, compiled by a committee of the National Council of Teachers of English (6th ed.); *About 100 Books: A Gateway to Better Intergroup Understanding*, for children from preschool to age sixteen, which includes Hispanic and Asian experiences; *The Child Immigrant: Establishing Roots in a New Country*, an annotated bibliography for the Association of Children's Librarians of Northern California's 1983 Institute program, which has "a list of vendors of foreign language materials" attached (order from: Joyce Simkins, 59 Duncan Way, Oakland, CA 94611, $5.00); *A Hispanic Heritage: A Guide to Juvenile Books about Hispanic People and Cultures*, by Isabel Schon; *LECTOR*, a journal published by The California Spanish Language Data Base,* which "reviews Spanish language and bilingual books as well as materials of Hispanic interest for both children and adults;" and *Bibliography: Children's Books from Asia 1980*, by the Asian Culture Center for UNESCO, which includes titles in English (order from ACCU, 6 Fukuromachi, Shinjuku-Ku, Tokyo 162, Japan, $6.00).

---

*According to *REFORMA Newsletter* 4 (Spring 1985): 11, "The California Spanish Language Data Base (CSLDB) has changed its name to: Hispanic Information Exchange (HISPANEX). Their services will include: SPANCAT a cataloging service that specializes in helping libraries catch up on their backlogs; *LECTOR* a bimonthly book review journal that features Spanish language book reviews written in English; COPAS an acquisition system for Spanish materials; and Floricanto, a publisher of reference materials and children's books. Write to: Vivian Pizano, HISPANEX, 604 William St., Oakland, CA 94612. Phone (415) 893–8702."

Ruth provides advice about finding reliable dealers of books in languages other than English. Among the sources recommended are the Information Center on Children's Cultures (United States Committee on Children's Cultures, Committee for UNICEF, 331 East 38th Street, New York, NY 10016); *Books in Other Languages: A Guide to Selection Aids and Suppliers*, by Leonard Wertheimer (Ottawa: Canadian Library Association, 1979); and The National Clearinghouse for Bilingual Education's *Guide to Publishers and Distributors Serving Minority Languages*, by Harpreet K. Sandhu and Laura A. Bukkila, rev. ed. (Rosslyn, Va.: National Clearinghouse for Bilingual Education, 1980).

* * *

Respondent role: County Librarian (response no. 4)

Selection guidelines—The Los Angeles County Public Library guidelines, *Materials Selection Policy and Practice*, are those used for selection of all materials, "including those for children of ethnic heritage." In addition, "The Children's book evaluator utilizes the criteria for analyzing children's books for racism and sexism put out by the Council on Interracial Books for Children."

Attachments included: (1) a copy of the Materials Selection Policy and Practices; (2) a copy of Selection Statement: Children's Materials (a portion of this latter document states, "Books in other languages are included both for children desiring to learn a new language and for children who wish to read in their first language"); (3) a brief list reflecting the content of "Ten Quick Ways to Analyze Children's Books for Racism and Sexism," a publication of the Council on Interracial Books for Children; (4) a page from the *Interracial Books for Children Bulletin* 7 (no. 4), 6 (this provides a list of "basic resources for consciousness-raising." Topics treated are related to institutional and cultural racism, sexism, third-world and feminist views, and book selection aids); (5) a page from the *Interracial Books for Children Bulletin* 7 (nos. 2 and 3), 4 entitled "Criteria for Analyzing Books on Asian-Americans" (topics treated include: concerns about realities and ways-of-life as actually lived by Asian American persons; ways in which content of materials should go beyond stereotypes; rectification of historical distortions and omissions; avoidance of treating Asian American minorities as if they are models to emulate; awareness of changing status of women; and accuracy in art and photography so as to show racial diversity of Asian-Americans); and (6) a memorandum from the Children's Book Evaluator to the Chief, Technical Services Division, wherein it is stated: "We strongly believe in the necessity of the involvement of representatives of target groups in the selection process. Staff from ethnic centers and / or the ethnic groups being addressed are called upon as advisers when a particular title is being considered."

The county librarian comments about the ethnic centers, "We are fortunate to have staff through our system who are bilingual (and bicultural) in Spanish or East Asian languages. They are called upon to assist both the Children's Book Evaluator and the Ethnic Materials Evaluator in reviewing materials. The ethnic centers mentioned in the attached memo from the Children's Book Evaluator refer to our Chicano Resources Center, Asian-Pacific Resources Center. Each is housed in a community library which serves large populations of the relevant group."

For additional information, write to Sylva N. Manoogian, Principal Librarian, Foreign Languages Department, Los Angeles Public Library, 630 West Fifth Street, Los Angeles, CA 90071.

* * *

Respondent role: Children's Book Evaluator (response no. 3) Selection guidelines — "Often ethnic and foreign materials do not measure up in terms of our general selection policy's description of acceptable format. These materials are still purchased when the content has value in terms of the recreational and information needs of the target group or in terms of general social significance for cultural awareness." Recommended lists and publishers' catalogs are shared by the children's book evaluator and the ethnic materials evaluator.

Inservice — "Staff members are expected to increase their awareness of the needs of specific groups through attendance at conferences, inservice training, and by regular reading of materials such as the *Interracial Books for Children Bulletin* and titles such as those in their reading list (attached). [Author's note: see item number (4) specified with attachments list above.] Children's service staff are instructed to be aware of the Council on Interracial Books for Children's "Ten Quick Ways to Analyze Books for Racism and Sexism" (attached) and are given copies during formal training for new librarians."

* * *

Respondent role: County Librarian (response no. 3)

Programming activities — Librarians at the resource centers, "in conjunction with the Minority Services Coordinator, . . . have presented programs for the enjoyment and education of staff and our public." A flyer which accompanied the attachments announces in Spanish and English that the public is invited to attend the third in a series of Latin authors and poets symposiums. Refreshments and book sales were to take place as well as the program. The program featured "Guest Speaker Javier Pacheco, Poet and Musicologist, Recipient of the Second Award, Fourth Annual Chicano Literary Prize, 1978, and published in numerous journals and periodicals and readings from their works by authors and poets, under the direction of Manuel 'Manazar' Gamboa, Director of Consilio de Arte Popular, Lindsey Haley-Aleman, Harry Gamboa, and Luis Rodriquez." The program was sponsored by the Library Foundation.

*　　*　　*

Respondent role: Outreach Services Coordinator (response no. 6).

The section on selection criteria in the library manual advises the selectors that some of the usual selection criteria are revised "because of the relative lack of published material by Chicano authors in the United States and the low variety of Spanish materials in some subject areas." Advice to selectors tells them not to be deterred by poor format if the material "is not available in other forms," or by "lack of inclusion in review media, bibliographies or indexes." A strong criterion is that of "popular interest and demand." Local Chicano materials, e.g., "including books, art, and films," should be acquired "for the interest and information they provide" and as "a means of preserving ethnic local history." The selectors are advised that "areas of high need in the Spanish-speaking community . . . include periodicals, audiovisual materials, picture books, light fiction and fiction by Latino authors, and Chicano and Mexican history and culture."

Additional selection criteria relative to the content of children's materials were concerned with: (1) "absence of racism" — materials purchased being "free from ethnic stereotypes and biases"; (2) "absence of sexism" — special care to be taken in examination of materials because (a) "many ethnic women feel that they face a double oppression, both as members of an ethnic group and as females," and (b) "materials published in other countries, where women may still have a more subordinate role, may be more blatantly sexist"; and (3) positive role models.

Added attachments were copies of "Ten Quick Ways to Analyze Children's Books for Racism" and a "Values Checklist," which had been used for a "Library Services for Bicultural Children Workshop" and which is reprinted on pages 77–80 of the 1979 publication *A Guide for Developing Ethnic Library Services*, developed by the California Ethnic Services Task Force. The "Materials Selection Policy" is based in large part upon the "Ten Quick Ways."

Inservice — "We incorporate sensitivity to various cultures into our workshops sponsored by the Affirmative Action Committee, such as the one on 'Sensitivity to Cultural Differences as Seen in the Interviewing Process,' which occurred in spring 1983. Workshops on storytelling for children address usage of Spanish and books reflecting Mexican culture. Our collection reflects primarily Mexican culture — with little indication of Cuban or Puerto Rican Spanish backgrounds. All workshops are attended by professional and paraprofessional staff. At this time we have twenty individuals receiving bilingual pay for usage of their Spanish."

Summary of Findings — Public Libraries, Central Region

1. Respondents to the requests for information about selection criteria, inservice, and other related matters for the seven public librarians included: two directors; two deputy librarians; three coordinators of childrens services; one head of a foreign language department; one head of a literature department. (In one instance, the responses of three individuals were attached and forwarded.)

2. Specific selection policies are stated which relate to the purchase of foreign language materials; materials to remove "prejudice and ignorance regarding racial, ethnic, or religious groups of people" and to "foster healthy attitudes", and materials to provide insight into "the human and social condition." Whenever possible, one library has books reviewed for accuracy "by a member of the particular national, religious or racial group involved." Another arranges for personnel to preview copies of Spanish books from distributors and book stores. Many librarians have no specialized policies. For one library, identification of suppliers for Asian materials is cited as a greater problem than development of criteria for selection.

   One library reports that the special bibliographies in the *Booklist* and the issues of the *Interracial Books for Children Bulletin* are useful for selection purposes.

3. One library contracts with community agencies and a university professor for inservice activities "related to ethnic and racial education and sensitivity"; another reports sharing inservice activities related to foreign languages with personnel of the local school district. A recently developed list of juvenile books in the Spanish Language and with Hispanic themes was forwarded by a library which is also planning an Asian booklist.

4. Recent programming was mentioned by two libraries; one library described the programming themes for Hispanic and Asian children; the other listed books used for library programs where children from Vietnam were present. In addition, one library described the responses made to Vietnamese patrons who seek to learn English as a second language and to children who study in bilingual programs or seek to do social studies reports.

EXCERPTS — PUBLIC LIBRARIES, CENTRAL REGION

Respondent role: Coordinator, Children's Services (response no. 10).

Selection guidelines — Books are purchased and cataloged for a foreign-language collection. "No separate criteria for this collection exists." The following considerations are made in the selection of materials; (1) attractiveness to "Hispanic and Asian groups as well as to children for whom English is their first language"; (2) inclusion of a variety of materials, e.g., "familiar stories translated into another language, bilingual books, dictionary-type or other word books by which articles can be identified"; (3) "neither the art nor the text should stereotype any group in any way."

Attached was a copy of a booklist of Hispanic books compiled in 1984 by the Children's Services Office. The list includes Spanish and English books with Hispanic themes. It will be made "available in all libraries, the International Center and the Hispano-American Center. An Asian booklist is planned for the future."

Inservice — "A staff meeting to emphasize foreign language materials in the adult collection" was planned by the Adult Services Office. Guests included an administrator from the local public school district staff and a high school teacher.

A program is being planned by the Children's Services Office for the 1984–85 year to stimulate "the interest of the staff in the juvenile foreign language collection. A guest speaker from the foreign language department of the local school district will be featured."

Program activities—"Library staff have annually participated in the International Festival, sponsored by the International Center, and the 'Fiesta,' sponsored by the public about materials and activities."

Two programs in the 1983–84 Sunday Kaleidoscope series for school-age children at the Central Library were on the following themes: Hispanic Holiday, featuring a guest from the Hispanic Center; and China Magic, featuring a guest from the community who has developed his skill in the old magic of China."

* * *

Respondent role: Deputy Librarian (response no. 11)

Selection guidelines—The metropolitan area is reported to have individuals who are "Asians as .001%" and "Hispanics as .0014%" of the population. Service has been provided "principally to (1) adult or young adult Vietnamese who are learning English through a special program by the local Travelers' Aid and (2) English-speaking children" in the bilingual program of the public schools.

Additional information is provided from attached reports provided by the Head of the Children's Department and the Head of the Literature Department.

* * *

Respondent role: Head, Literature Department (response no. 11)

Selection guidelines—The same criteria are used for all materials.

The library has been unable to find a supplier to meet the demand for Cambodian materials. "Our biggest problem is not developing criteria for collection development but rather to find someone to supply the titles we want."

* * *

Respondent role: Head, Children's Department (response no. 11)

Selection guidelines: Selection aids used to supplemental the book selection policy of the public library include: "*Booklist*—special bibliographies—e.g., 'Spanish Language Books for Young Children,' and the *Interracial Books for Children Bulletin.*

"The Children's Department served as an important resource when Travelers' Aid was teaching English library skills, etc. to newly arrived Vietnamese. We did notice the Vietnamese students responded quite excitedly to books about their country.

"Demands for books in Spanish and about Spanish-speaking people come mostly from students" in the public schools "and from students with Social Studies assignments on these cultures." Inservice—Patrons have been referred to the Children's Department from the Literature Department "for books on Vietnam or books in English and Vietnamese."

Program activities—"We have recommended books from our collection to be used in branch programs attended by Vietnamese children. Some titles are: Vuong, *The Brocaded Slipper*; Pomerantz, *The Princess and the Admiral*; Tanka, *The Tortoise and the Sword*; and other collections of folklore and books by Jacqueline Ayer."

Summary of Findings—Public Libraries, Eastern Region

1. Respondents to the requests for information about selection criteria, inservice, and other matters related to the present publication for the seven public libraries included: one director; one deputy director; one coordinator of youth services; one children's coordinator, one chief librarian of children's and schools department; one head of book selection, office of work with children; one head of book selection, office of work with adults / young adults; one children's materials specialist.

2. One respondent indicated that in many cases books for minority children (especially those in another language) are so scarce that they are acquired simply because they were available.

   A second respondent indicates that the usual criteria used to evaluate format and quality of illustration have to be relaxed somewhat for some materials in other languages.

   A third respondent relies on the library's reviews: although books are sought which exhibit "non-stereotypic and non-propagandistic attitudes," some new editions of classics or older titles that reflect beliefs of former times may be acceptable. Two respondents indicate that materials by Hispanic and Asian authors in their languages are preferred to titles written in English which have been translated in order, as one respondent indicated, to encourage readers to "retain an interest and facility in both their language and their culture."

   A fourth respondent indicates that several Spanish-speaking bilingual staff members contribute their knowledge to the selection process.

3. One library is reported to have had staff workshops on book selection in general. Another library reports that inservice activity has

related to the publication of book lists. A third library indicates that one of the primary purposes for inservice training of the staff has been to develop multicultural awareness.

4. One library indicates that the programming activities, especially in Spanish, are predominantly "storytelling, dramatics and puppets."

EXCERPTS — PUBLIC LIBRARIES, EASTERN REGION

Respondent role: Head, Book Selection, Office of Work with Children; Head, Book Selection, Office of Work with Adults / Young Adults (response no. 17)

Selection guidelines — From the policy statement entitled "Foreign Language Children's Books in the Central Children's Department, Policies and Procedures for Selecting and Ordering, Revised September 1977," a respondent indicates that the following are objectives: (1) to develop balanced representation in all areas of the world (with exception of English-speaking countries); (2) to give priority to picture and easy-reading books except those in "the most prominent languages"; (3) to acquire books from preschool to sixth grade reading level "in the most prominent languages (Spanish, French, German, Italian)"; (4) to purchase major award books, e.g., the Mildred Batchelder award, in the original languages; and Batchelder Award, (5) to acquire books in original languages in preference to translations of titles originally written in English.

* * *

Respondent role: Director (response no. 18)

Inservice: "The in-service training for our staff has been designed primarily to enhance multicultural awareness. For example, a local artist, Ms. Michele Valeri, recently shared her experience traveling and studying in Latin America with our children's staff. Ms. Valeri has written and performed music for children which can successfully be used in library programs. *Mi Casa Es Su Casa* is a recorded 'bilingual musical journey' which can transport both Spanish-speaking and non-Spanish-speaking children to new places. Demonstrating ways for librarians to initiate this experience is the goal of such training."

* * *

Respondent role: Materials Specialist (response no. 15)

Inservice: "Basic inservice activity relating to this material is the publication of booklists 'Libros en Español' (currently under revision) and 'The Chinese in Children's Books' (schedules to be revised this year to include all Asian languages presently in our collections). Our focus is, as noted, on material produced by the culture over translations." Copies of the two lists were enclosed.

Summary of Findings — School District Library Supervisors

1. Respondents to the requests for information about selection criteria, inservice, and other matters for the eight school district library supervisors are: two supervisors of media services; one director of school libraries; one district coordinator of library services; one supervisor of library services; one media coordinator; one media specialist; and one unknown (informal note attached).
2. Three respondents report evaluation forms for examining material for ethnic content. One library's evaluation questions drew upon the "Ten Quick Ways to Analyze Children's Books for Sexism and Racism," by the Council on Interracial Books for children.
3. Inservice in one school district utilizes lists of authors and writers based on *Something About the Author*, a multi-ethnic bibliography, and a multicultural list of easy-to-read books. In another district there is a list of suggested activities for ESOL and bilingual students which has been used for inservice. A third district has had persons from the Council on Interracial Books for Children twice as inservice speakers concerning stereotyping.
4. Agencies and materials which may be useful as sources of information are suggested by three respondents.

EXCERPTS — SCHOOL DISTRICTS LIBRARIES

Respondent role: Supervisor, Media Services (response no. 21) An Ethnic Content Review Form and a Sex Balance Review Form are used in the Seattle Public Schools. Ratings on the ten-item scale of the Ethnic Content Review Form must be documented by reference to page numbers.

The first four items must be checked "yes" or "no" with respect to adverse reflections concerning: (1) ethnic stereotyping / racism in (a) illustrations, (b) language, and (c) life styles; (2) differences in customs or life styles being shown as undesirable; (3) material being limited to the root culture; and (4) depiction of diverse ethnic groups being proportionally accurate if material is about contemporary American society.

The other six items concern accurate portrayal of roles; (5) fair proportions of minority and majority characters being shown in "mentally active, creative, and problem-solving roles"; (6) minority individuals being shown in nontraditional roles as well as the ones to which society has usually restricted them; (7) fair proportions of minority and majority individuals in "(a) Professional, (b) Executive and (c) Vocational" roles; (8) "achievements in art, science, or any other field" presenting contributions of minority persons; (9) historically accurate imbalances or inequalities being interpreted "in light of contemporary standards and circumstances" in student material; and (10) ethnic information and guidance being provided in teacher instruction so as to reflect awareness that teachers' multi-ethnic contacts vary.

A cumulative rating form is provided with spaces for the names of the individuals who perform the ratings and the schools where each is employed. A half-page narrative summary for ethnic content and sex balance can be filled out by the chairperson of the committee. A copy is enclosed of the "Ten Quick Ways to Analyze Children's Books for Racism and Sexism,[11] the text of "which originally appeared in the *Bulletin* of the Council on Interracial Books for Children (Vol. 5, 1974)."

* * *

Respondent role: Media Coordinator (response no. 22)

Selection guidelines—A rating form entitled "Ethnic and Sexism Evaluation Tool' is used in the public schools. The ten items are similar to those of the Ethnic Content Review form of the Seattle Public Schools with the addition of words relating to sex roles for the first three questions. Questions four through nine correspond, with the addition of sex roles, to questions five to ten of the Seattle Public Schools. Question ten on the Portland Evaluation Tool relates to balanced proportions of sensitivity displayed by minority and non-minority male and female characters. The Portland checklist is reprinted from the 3 November 1974 issue of the *Bulletin of the Interracial Books for Children*.

Inservice—A copy of a memorandum to library media personnel dated 11 January 1984 provided for Human Relations Month a list of writers and illustrators of Afro-American and Asian-American children's books based on information "gathered from the Gale Research reference source, *Something About the Author*."

Copies of two other lists were provided also: "Chinese American, Japanese American and Asian American Multi-Ethnic Bibliography," prepared in January 1977, and "Multicultural Books for Primary," which is described as "a multicultural list of picture books and easy-to-read titles prepared for preschool and primary grade teachers" in October 1981. Subdivisions of the second list are African, Asian, Black, Chinese, Hispanic, Mexican, and Native American. It is noted from the annotations that books about American children of a given heritage are listed under some of the headings with books about stories which concern experiences of children in other countries.

* * *

Respondent role: Supervisor, Library Services (response no. 23)

Copies are provided of selection criteria used in the School District for Ethnic Groups and of the District Compliance Evaluation Form.

In the selection criteria, the selector is advised: The content of instructional materials relating to cultural minorities should be varied and should concern all social, economic, and educational levels of society. It should reflect recent findings of research and show cultural groups as a part of American pluralistic society.

Additional directions acknowledge that a librarian may have difficulty in applying all guidelines, "since many people are themselves not fully aware of the values and cultural contributions of specific ethnic groups and may not yet have developed a full sensibility to materials which either offend or denigrate others." Thus, the selector is advised to find a review or evaluation by a person with knowledge of the specific culture as well as of the subject of the material.

Criteria for "selection of materials on specific ethnic groups" include eleven general concerns and six questions about content and authorship. The general questions relate to potential effects of the materials on a student as well as their realistic and unbiased content. The questions relate to ways the material helps to: (1) develop appreciation for dignity and worthiness of all persons; (2) teach a person to value his or her own heritage; (3) "promote a positive self image"; (4) to show accurately participation of minorities in all aspects of American life, whether historical or contemporary; (5) show both sides of an issue or concern; (6) give frank treatment to "unresolved intercultural problems in the United States, including those which involve prejudice and discrimination"; (7) resolve possible conflict among a person's own values through examination of ethnic values expressed; (8) evaluate the culture depicted in terms of the values of that culture rather than the values of another culture; (9) counteract stereotypes and bias; (10) show characters "with strengths and weaknesses, who act in response to their own nature and times"; and (11) show characters "in situations consistent with the life styles of the culture."

The questions on content and authorship relate to: (1) the author's or producer's qualifications relative to the cultural group depicted; (2) the impartiality of nonfictional materials; (3) the possibility of ideas in fiction assisting a "reader in evaluating people and their actions"; (4) illustrations showing ethnic ways of living consistent with contemporary realities; (5) the suitability of content to "age, maturity, and experience" of intended readers; and (6) content stimulating additional "reading and investigation."

The District Compliance Evaluation Form requires that materials: (1) encourage "humane treatment of . . . people; (2) accurately show roles and contributions of "ethnic and cultural groups to the total development of California and the United States"; (3) not reflect "adversely upon persons because of their race, color, creed, national origin, ancestry, sex or occupation."

Inservice—A three-page list entitled "Library Activities for ESOL and Bilingual Students" suggests twelve groups of activities to be used in libraries or library-style classroom centers. "All the activities relate to library skill learnings, literature appreciation, or reading enrichment."

The activities include:

1. you-tell-the-story books—illustrated books without text provide reading readiness and motivation for creative writing. Stories may be recorded or written bilingually;
2. help-tell-the-story books—stories evoke participation and response by students. Books may be used to motivate creative writing and prepare plays, and for oral language activities;
3. alphabet books—reinforce communication and library locational skills through a variety of alphabet book activities, for example, creating original bilingual alphabet books;
4. Picture dictionaries—reinforce vocabulary and reference skills, create illustrated bilingual dictionaries, and match pictures, and folklore characters, for instance, with words.

Other suggestions describe activities for:

5. cumulative stories;
6. storytelling;
7. dramatizing;
8. centers, library style: (a) locational and library skills center, (b) listening / viewing center (cut-and-paste, write or tell about exciting, humorous, or interesting episode), (c) recording center (recordings may include translations, reviews, books, or pupils' stories), (d) recreational reading center (highlighting bilingual / bicultural materials and those in a language other than English), (e) author's workshop center, and (f) creative arts workshop center;
9. book jackets;
10. puzzles and games (emphasis on literary activities);
11. bilingual lessons; and
12. consult ESOL and bilingual teachers.

Although the list of activities was developed for in-service use with elementary teachers and librarians, the activities described may be adapted to enhance cultural and bilingual learning by children in public and school libraries as well as in classrooms.

* * *

Respondent role: District Coordinator, Library Services (response no. 24)

Selection guidelines — The language collection in North Carolina is mentioned as a useful source of information. (The authors assume that the foreign-language collection mentioned is North Carolina Foreign Language Center, Cumberland County Public Library, 328 Gillespie Street, Fayetteville, N.C. 28301.)

* * *

Respondent role: Media Specialist (response no. 25)

Selection — No information provided.

This school system has not received refugee families, but foreign children who speak English with minimum skill are enrolled in the school system fairly regularly.

Each child is approached informally on an individual basis. A phrase book was ordered immediately through interlibrary loan for a seventh-grade student from another country who was enrolled recently.

Inexpensive phrase books were ordered also for the teachers of the student. A guidance counselor sought help from students prior to the new classmate's arrival, and the students were eager to provide assistance. Several developed good rapport with the new student right away. The student was introduced to computers in the learning center and assigned a tutor. On the first day, the library media specialist provided several books with many pictures of the student's country and surrounding countries. The student seemed pleased to see familiar scenes.

For students from other countries, the media specialist says, "I try to find outside reading books for their assignments which have some meaning for them from their culture and which are not complicated prose. *Travels with Charley* by Steinbeck has been popular; *My Antonia* and Howard Fast's *The Hessian* have also been used with success."

Helpful selection tools have been *Reading Ladders for Human Relations*, by Dr. Eileen Tway, National Council of Teachers of English, and *The Book-Finder*, volumes 1 and 2, by Sharon Spredemann Dreyer, American Guidance Services.

A note is added from a high school librarian friend who has been active with a group of church women who organized a program to teach English to East Asian refugees. The friend gives several useful addresses of organizations with special teaching methods and materials:

> Booth Hoffman
> Volunteers of America
> 3813 N. Causeway Blvd.
> Metairie, La. 70002

> Literacy Volunteers of America
> 404 Oak Street
> Syracuse, N.Y. 13203

> Laubach Literacy Action
> New Readers Press
> 1320 Jamesville Avenue
> Syracuse, N.Y. 13210

She says: "The New Readers Press will be glad to send you their catalog. They publish both the *Laubach Way to Reading*, a series of five books especially designed for teaching English-speaking adults to read, and the *Laubach Way to English* ESOL (English for Speakers of Other Languages) material, plus many supplementary materials."

> Lutheran Church Women
> 2900 Queen Lane
> Philadelphia, Pa. 19129

"Martha Lane has been the moving spirit in developing both the ESOL material and *Emergency English for Refugees*. This helps immigrants to gain the necessary skills to start functioning rapidly in our society. *The Laubach Way to English* is used as the basic student material for the ESOL program, which is a slower and more thorough approach than is the *Emergency English* material."

CONCLUSIONS DRAWN FROM THE SURVEY

The overall message of the twenty-eight responses is that both school and public librarians need to seek more diligently (and the producing agencies to promote more effectively) resource information on materials for and about the designated cultural groups. The majority of the librarians queried are conscious of the need to pay attention to, to be aware of, matters of bias and stereotype, but there is as yet very little fine tuning of this awareness in terms of offering positive values for *all* American children and young people in materials for and about Hispanic and Asian-Pacific cultures.

It is evident that one of the best-known purveyors of criteria and guidelines for eliminating stereotyping and bias—the Council on Interracial Books for Children—is respected and influential, since fully one-quarter of the respondents knew their materials and used them. The excellent and off-revised *Reading Ladders for Human Relations* lists of books, now edited for the National Council of Teachers of English by Eileen Tway, is also known and trusted, but there should be more lists like it to provide assistance in even more directions. Trusted sources for purchase of books and other materials plus sources of culturally reliable reviews are also an evident need.

As to inservice education of librarians and library staff which they can in turn spin off in assisting teachers, parents, and other community workers, it seems that some outlines and patterns for workshops, and other programs—face to face and through the media—would be useful. There are some efforts being made, but as with nearly all staff development or continuing education efforts for the library professional, they are sporadic, generally unsequenced, and not totally satisfactory.

Finally, on a positive note, librarians and library media specialists show real concern for the effects materials have on children. There is increased awareness of the long-range damaging effects of bias and stereotype on the self-esteem and self-identity of the youth of the minority / migrant group, as well as on the attitudes and social adjustments of the majority-society members. Librarians have shown their willingness to adapt their standard selection and acquisition policies and procedures to the needs and realities of acquiring relevant materials for and about Hispanic and Asian people. They have shown initiative and persistence — some, even, an eagerness — to venture into unfamiliar languages, to search for hard-to-find sources and suppliers. Above all, they have demonstrated a desire to learn about cultural sensitivities, and, if necessary, to work to modify their own attitudes and perceptions. This survey, on the whole, provided encouragement for all who would persist in these efforts.

Chapter 6
Change, Guidelines, and Selected Resource Centers

THE CHALLENGE OF CHANGE

Response to change is frequently uneven in the best of circumstances. In 1975, Margaret R. Marshall observed that library services to teenagers who are either multiracial or immigrants differ in quality and quantity as they are provided by school libraries or public libraries.[1] She pointed out that while schools have a legal requirement to serve various categories of persons with specialized services, public libraries can and do vary widely in their provision of services. They may in actual practice range from apathy and lack of materials for young people in general and those with special needs in particular, to careful assessment of need and provision of materials and services.

Although librarians may be alert to needs of their users, Leona Daniels says, "Dependence upon demand creating supply" should not be the only approach to the identification of materials.[2] Daniels declares, "It can be demonstrated that supply invites demand. Librarians must accept the challenge and create a reading interest by supplying the titles." Although Daniels speaks here about the Jewish minority culture being represented in children's fiction, her remarks are equally applicable to the representation of other minority cultures.

Some librarians have modified policies in order to facilitate the rapid acquisition of needed materials. Nathan A. Josel, Director of El Paso Public Libraries in Texas, describes a selection policy whereby each librarian within the library, including the director, participates in the selection process.[3] A sum of money is credited to each selector for the development of the collections. A coordinator of main library services, aided by a committee, monitors the titles selected for currency and appropriateness. Committee members include branch, technical services, and main library representatives.

Selection procedures for Spanish-language materials vary from those followed for selection of English-language materials for the following reasons:

1. Few standard reviewing tools exist for Spanish-language materials.
2. Those tools which do exist are usually incomplete and compiled late in the publishing process.
3. Publications in Spain and Mexico are not available over the long term. *Now* is the only time an available title may be obtained.
4. Bibliographic control for individual titles and series is less precise than for many North American publishers; variations of the same title may be issued by several publishers at approximately the same time.[4]

For the reasons given above, El Paso Public Library produced a general bibliography of currently available titles for North American libraries, *La Lista* (vol. I, no. 1), which is sent in 1982 to other selected libraries to determine the potential market for such a list. As a result, *La Lista* may now be subscribed to by forwarding $15.00 with the request to subscribe to El Paso Public Libraries. In 1985, 100 titles available for purchase are listed, including those for school-age children as well as adults pursuing graduate study. Clearly, this purchasing list is potentially useful for both public and school libraries. In additon, Josel advocates that librarians subscribe to LECTOR, produced by the California Spanish Language Data Base (Vivian Pizano, HISPANEX, 604 William St., Oakland, CA 94612. Tel. 415-893-8702). This journal was also recommended by Grace Ruth in Chapter V for its reviews of Spanish-language and bilingual books and materials of Hispanic interest.

El Paso Public Library works closely with Spanish-language jobbers "to identify rapidly and to purchase quickly" materials which are to be added to the Spanish-language collection.[5] Josel emphasizes that the bulk of the Spanish-language materials are purchased before they are submitted to the Spanish-language selection committee for analysis, review, and recommendation. Many of the materials are purchased by genre, e.g., *fotonovelas* (heavily illustrated light reading comparable to Harlequins) and *revistas* (popular periodicals "analogous to *Seventeen, Better Homes and Gardens*, and *Mademoiselle*").

Josel states that the acceptance rate of the Spanish-language materials purchased after completion of the review process has been 90 percent, so the process of "buy first, evaluate later" has proven to be cost effective. The primary value, of course, is ability to respond to the needs of so many Spanish-language readers.[6]

Proyecto LEER, an acronym for *L* ibros *E* lementales *E* ducativos y *R* ecreativos, provides information and assistance to those persons who select materials in Spanish for children and young adults.[7] To be placed on the mailing list for the *Proyecto LEER Bulletin*, write to the Texas Woman's University, School of Library Science, P.O. Box 22905, TWU Station, Denton, Tex. 76204. *Proyecto LEER Bulletin* 16 (Fall 1980) states the mission and services of Proyecto LEER as being:

- "to evaluate and review educational and recreational materials in Spanish;
- to train librarians and teachers in selection and acquisition of materials for the Spanish-speaking through courses and workshops;
- to disseminate information on these processes, and other materials and programs of interest to the Spanish-speaking;
- to work with libraries, schools, community programs and commercial distributors to make available information about these materials."

These objectives constituted the original mission of Proyecto LEER when it was located in Washington, D.C. When it was relocated to the TWU School of Library Science, in Texas, additional objectives included:

- "creation of the first evaluation and research center in library education to focus on examination of the information needs and reading patterns of the Spanish-speaking,
- development of an expanding data base of research results, reading interests of the Spanish-speaking including library users, non-users, services and resources
- offering of advisory services to individuals and organizations wishing to initiate and / or improve library services for the Spanish-speaking."

Marie Zielinska, director of the Multilingual Biblioservice, National Library of Canada (MBS), has shared a copy of their *Book Selection Guidelines*, revised in January 1983: "MBS selects, acquires, and catalogues books in the non-official languages spoken in Canada. These books are then made available on a long-term basis to public libraries throughout Canada."[8] The book collections, in twenty-seven languages, are designed to be nonscholarly but representative of a wide range of tastes and interests.

After studying the needs of users, guidelines have been devised "to assist language specialists, book selectors, and occasionally, book suppliers." The types of books being sought are those: (1) "for leisure reading, NOT for credit-oriented study or academic research"; (2) "representing a variety of outlooks and opinions, but NOT those which present extreme political views or contain religious or racial attacks or are polemical in character"; (3) "of good taste, NOT books which encourage or glorify violence, brutality or drug abuse and NOT books of pornography"; (4) "reflecting the cultural characteristics of the people in whose language the book is written, but NOT those containing mainly propaganda or advertising material"; and (5) "newly published . . . and original works" in preference "to old editions and translations."

Sixty-five percent of the acquisitions are "fiction, both novels and short stories": (1) "mostly popular, quality contemporary works for adults"; (2) "classics which are still in popular demand by the general reading public, particularly attractive, and illustrated editions"; and (3) translations . . . limited to classics and best sellers."

Twenty percent of the acquisitions are to be "books for children up to age ten." Well-illustrated books are preferred. Unacceptable are "books with crossword puzzles, cut-outs, or pages for coloring, books with sound recording or picture books without text."

Fifteen percent of the acquisitions are designed to be subject-oriented works in various categories which reflect "an ethnic culture directly related to the language of writing." Categories which had restrictions were: (1) "folklore, but NOT ethnology"; (2) "readers with vocabularies, but NOT grammar books with exercises"; (3) "no dictionaries or language-study materials unless specifically requested"; and (4) "no literary criticism, unless of a general nonscholarly nature, possibly with biographical accounts."

Other guidelines are specified for the physical format, numbers of copies which are desired and unit costs which will be permitted. Inquiries about these guidelines or other practices may be forwarded to the National Library of Canada, Multilingual Biblioservice, 395 Wellington Street, Ottawa, Ontario, Canada K1A ON4.

These guidelines are used flexibly. They are quoted here to illustrate that general guidelines about the nature of materials to be acquired can be quite specific in terms of user needs. Although few libraries in the United States purchase the amounts of materials acquired by the National Library of Canada, the approach to acquisition is similar to that of El Paso Public Libraries in that, in some instances, materials must be acquired as they become available prior to any reviewing procedures.

A source of reviews and lists about resource centers is *Focus on Asian Studies*, "a magazine created to reach out to educators, professionals, and Asia buffs looking for a comprehensive source journal on Asia.[9] Eight dollars (or $11.00 for persons outside the United States), by check or money order made out to the Asia Society, Inc., and mailed to FOCUS, P.O. Box 1308-M, Fort Lee, N.J. 07024, will start a one-year subscription of this journal, which is published three times a year. Many of the materials reviewed will make useful additions to historical and biographical collections for children and young people, and educators will find sources for model curricula and multimedia materials to use in teaching. Public libraries may find the lists of cultural events, e.g., museums, concerts, and art tours, useful for their users.

Phyllis J. Kimura Hayashibara has a useful list of selected sources for materials that includes several school districts which have produced curricular materials. The source list is attached to her article "A Guide to Bilingual Instructional Materials for Speakers of Asian and Pacific Island Languages", which has information concerning Vietnamese materials in AMERASIA Journal 5 (1978): 101-14. A list of outreach centers is in *Focus on Asian Studies* 1 (Fall 1983): 27. In *Asia: Teaching About / Learning From*, Seymour Fersh lists many resources.

Changes in society may lead to more reviewing aids and information resource centers to consult in this field. In like manner, additional sources of criteria for selection of materials can be sought from state agencies and the professional literature. An excellent example of the latter is "Criteria for Evaluation of Ethnic Materials" by Wendell Wray which is in *Ethnic Collections in Libraries*.[10]

SELF-CONCEPT AND LANGUAGE MAINTENANCE

Encouragement for development of healthy self-concepts by children and young people is an important objective of librarians and educators. Elimination of bias and stereotypes is one approach; accuracy and honesty in culturally relevant materials is another. A third is related to language maintenance, for which are needed materials to support and maintain the skill of those persons who are bilingual and multilingual.

Bilingual education has a longer history in the United States than people usually stop to realize. Multilingualism and cultural pluralism has been characteristic of our country from its earliest times. Colonial languages, spoken by the European colonizers from the sixteenth through the eighteenth centuries, included English, Spanish, French, German, Russian, Swedish, and Dutch. Joshua A. Fishman indicated in the 1960s that there were approximately "three hundred recognizably separate American Indian languages and dialects still being spoken."[11] Hayashibara states that bilingual education was so common at one time "that nine million people had been taught in both German and English before 1910."[12]

All through the great immigration waves of the early twentieth century and afterward, there were millions of people in the United States who spoke two or more languages. However, in the rush to assimilation of the "melting-pot" days, there was not always pride in speaking the mother tongue of one self or one's parents, nor desire to maintain fluent use of it.

With the human, civil, and cultural rights ferment of the 1960s, attitudes toward language changed. Parents wanted children to maintain their language of origin, not to replace it with English. For millions and for generations there has been one language spoken in home and neighborhood, and another—English—spoken in school, or sometimes, but not always, on the job. Still, English, the official language of the country, must be learned if success in the wider world outside the cultural circle were to be attained.

Known to many as "the bilingual education act of 1968," Title VII was added to the Elementary and Secondary Education Act in that year. It was designed primarily to promote—in fact, to make possible— proficiency and learning in English for children for whom English was a second language.[13] It was not enacted to promote bilingualism, but it was seized upon to serve that purpose, especially by the increasingly politically aware and growing Spanish-speaking populations in the big-city school districts. Reauthorized in 1974, 1978, and again in 1984 as Title II of the Educational Amendments Act (PL-98-511), the law providing transitional learning from the language of home to the official language of country continues to operate, variously interpreted, to the benefit of millions of cultural minority and immigrant children. It is authorized through 1988. Information is available about almost any aspect of bilingual education from the National Clearinghouse for Bilingual Education by means of its toll-free hotline: (800) 336-4560. A monthly newsletter, *Forum*, is available at no charge.

Federally sponsored resource centers exist to support educators, educational administrators, and librarians in their quest for materials. The following list is made available by the National Clearinghouse for Bilingual Education for 1986. The clearinghouse can mail free-of-charge lists of publishers of materials by designated cultural groups from its online data base REPUB. In addition, it can provide bibliographies of criteria for selecting materials, reprints of articles related to material selection, and online search services. These resource centers have information and services which are important for educators and librarians (public as well as school) who are not directly involved in bilingual education. The list of Bilingual Education Multifunctional Support Centers includes:

New England Bilingual Education
    Multifunctional Support Center
345 Blackstone Boulevard
Brown University, Potter Building
Providence, R.I. 02906
(401) 274-9548
Director: Adeline Becker
Service Area 1: Connecticut, Maine,
    Massachusetts, New Hampshire,
    Rhode Island, Vermont

New York State Bilingual
    Multifunctional Support Center
Hunter College of CUNY
695 Park Avenue, Box 367
New York, N.Y. 10021
(212) 772-4764

Director: José Váquez
Service Area 2: New York

Georgetown University Bilingual Education Service Center
(GUBESC)
2139 Wisconsin Avenue, N.W. Suite 100
Washington, D.C. 20007
(202) 625-3540
Director: Ramón Santiago
Service Area 3: Delaware, District of Columbia, Maryland,
New Jersey, North Carolina, Ohio, Pennsylvania Virginia,
West Virginia

Bilingual Education South Eastern Support Center (BESES)
Florida International University
School of Education TRMO3
Tamiami Campus
Miami, Fla. 33199
(305) 554-2962; 800 432-1406 (in Florida);
(800) 325-6002 (rest of region)
Director: Rosa Inclán
Service Area 4: Alabama, Florida, Georgia, Kentucky,
Mississippi, South Carolina, Tennessee

Midwest Bilingual Education Multifunctional Resource Center
2360 East Devon Avenue, Suite 3011
Des Plaines, Ill. 60018
(312) 296-6070
Director: Minerva Coyne
Service Area 5: Illinois, Indiana, Iowa, Michigan, Missouri,
Minnesota, North Dakota, South Dakota, Wisconsin

Region 6 Bilingual Education Multifunctional Support Center
Texas A & I University
Campus Box 136
Kingsville, Tex. 78363
(512) 595-3788
Director: María Barrera
Service Area 6: Texas—Education Service Center Regions I
through IV, XX

Bilingual Education Training and Technical Assistance
(BETTA) Network

Universiy of Texas at El Paso
El Paso, Tex. 79968
(915) 747-5524
Director: Ernest Pérez
Service Area 7: Arkansas, Louisiana, Oklahoma, Texas—
Education Service Center Regions V through XIX

BUENO Bilingual Education Multifunctional Support Center
University of Colorado
School of Education
Campus Box 249
Boulder, Colo. 80309
(303) 492-5416
Director: Rodolfo Chávez
Service Area 8: Colorado, Kansas, Nebraska,
New Mexico, Utah

Interface Educational Network
7080 S.W. Fir Loop, Suite 200
Portland, Oreg. 97223
(503) 684-0584
Director: Esther Puentes
Service Area 9: Alaska, Idaho, Oregon, Montana, Washington,
Wyoming

SDSU—Multifunctional Support Center
San Diego State University
6363 Alvarado Court, Suite 200
San Diego, Calif. 92120
(619) 265-5193
Director: William Adorno
Service Area 10: Arizona—non-Indian programs; California—
counties of Imperial, Orange, Riverside, San Bernardino,
San Diego

Bilingual Education Multifunctional Support Center—LA
California State University
5151 State University Drive
Los Angeles, Calif. 90032
(213) 224-3676
Director: Charles F. Leyba

Service Area 11: California—counties of Los Angeles, Santa Barbara, Ventura

Bilingual Education Multifunctional Support Center
National Hispanic University
255 East 14th Street
Oakland, Calif. 94606
(415) 451-0511
Director: Roberto Cruz
Service Area 12: California—all counties north of and including San Luis Obispo, Kern, and Inyo; Nevada

Bilingual Education Multifunctional Support Center
Colegio Universitario Metropolitano
P.O. Box CUM
Rio Piedras, P.R. 00928
(809) 766-1717
Director: César D. Cruz Cabello
Service Area 13: Commonwealth of Puerto Rico, Virgin Islands

Hawaii American Samoa Multifunctional Resource Center
1150 South King St. #203
Honolulu, Hawaii 97814
(808) 531-7502
Director: Helen R. Nagtalon-Miller
Service Area 14: American Samoa, Hawaii

Project BEAM (Bilingual Education Assistance in Micronesia)
University of Guam, College of Education
UOG Station
Mangilao, Guam 96923
Cable: "Univ Guam"; telex: 721-6275
International telephone: (671) 734-4113
Director: Robert Underwood
Service Area 15: Commonwealth of Northern Mariana Islands, Guam, Trust Territory of the Pacific Islands

National Indian Bilingual Center
Community Services Building
Arizona State University
Tempe, Ariz. 85287

(602) 965-5688
Director: Karen Swisher
Service Area 16: Alaska, Arizona, California, Michigan,
Minnesota, Montana, New Mexico, North Carolina,
Oklahoma, South Dakota, Utah, Washington, Wyoming 14

Forwarded from one of these bilingual education centers is an interesting article in response to the authors' inquiries entitled "Selecting and Evaluating a Textbook."[15] A detailed checklist is used in the rating process. Daoud and Celce-Murcia say, "If a distinction can be maintained between . . . the recording of data and the evaluation of the same, subjective error, which is often the reason for difference of opinion among raters, can be minimized to a great extent."[16]

Persons who are interested in systematizing the process of evaluating materials may wish to examine the Daoud / Celce-Murcia process of surveying, analyzing, and judging. The procedures and some items of the checklist may suggest similar systematic analyses which could be established for the evaluating of other types of materials.

The lists of preliminary data included in the article may be useful for teachers and librarians to consider as they evaluate library materials for use by children and young adults. The student background information, e.g., age range, proficiency level in English, and background languages, can be useful information about any group of potential users.

Other bibliographies representative of the types of materials available at the bilingual centers have been prepared from the library holdings of the Midwest Bilingual Education Multifunctional Support Center in Arlington Heights, Illinois. Some of the information contained in the bibliographies is useful for schools and libraries which have no bilingual studies. Volume I contains Spanish-language materials, including materials for teaching Spanish as a second language.[17]

Volume II contains content area materials in Spanish and English (content areas being math, science, social studies, early childhood, interdisciplinary, fine arts, and other, e.g., human development and career education). The title of Volume II is *Curriculum Materials for Bilingual and Multicultural Education: An Annotated Bibliography.* Preschool through adult materials, printed and audiovisual, are included. In addition to title and author, ratings are provided concerning the interest, reading, and language levels of each material listed. Components of each item are indicated, e.g., number of pages in the text or supplementary book, number of workbook pages, languages used in the teacher's guide, existence of tests in the material, and indication of format of materials other than books, e.g. cassette, film, flash card, manipulative, or record. The name of the publisher, year, and edition are given.[18]

In the introduction to Volume I, María Medina Swanson, director of the Bilingual Education Support Center, describes the purpose of the annotated bibliography: "The library's aim is to help programs and individuals involved in bilingual and multicultural education identify and select materials which best meet their needs. To facilitate this process, an annotated bibliography of the library's holdings has been developed. In addition to providing a representative sampling of available materials, this bibliography will assist in the preliminary selection of instructional and inservice tools. The bibliography is divided into curriculum areas following the library classification system, and consequently, will also aid library users in identifying and locating materials at the Resource Library."[19]

An example of an annotation from the first volume is: "*Fantasia Boricua*, María Teresa Barín — This collection of short prose selections presents the author's memories of her childhood in Puerto Rico. Excellent graphics.[20] This is a 170-page book with interest level from eleventh grade to adult. Reading level is adult. Language level is advanced. The publisher is Instituto de Cultura Puertorriqueño, San Juan de Puerto Rico. Date of publication is 1973.

An example of an annotation from the second volume is: "*Borinquen before Columbus*, Mary Segarra de Bíaz et al. — This text provided a cultural description of the Taíno Indians — their origins, physical characteristics, social structure, agriculture, weapons and defense, and religion. Also included are a vocabulary list of indigenous words, a bibliography, and a brief historical account of Diego Salcedo. Spanish and English texts are presented side by side, with Taíno vocabulary words underlined for emphasis. Oversized, softcover book."[21] The interest level is from grades three to five. The reading level from grades five to six. The language level is advanced. There are forty-one pages. The publisher is Los Amigos del Museo del Barrio, Inc., 1945 Third Avenue, New York, N.Y. 10029. There is no date of publication listed. The folk music recordings listed in Volume II include those of many countries, e.g., Mexico, Philippines, Peru, Southwest Asia, and Japan.[22]

In 1978, Rudolph C. Troike examined research for evidence of the effectiveness of bilingual education and concluded "that a quality bilingual education program can be effective in meeting the goals of equal educational opportunity for minority language children. . . ."[23] Muriel Saville-Troike recommends "reliable resources" about bilingualism in *Bilingual Children: A Resource Document.*[24]

In 1982, Iris C. Rotberg indicated that "a World Bank review of selected international case studies found that 'there is not one answer to the question of what language to use for primary school, but several answers, depending on the characteristics of the child, of the parents and the local community.'"[25] This view concerning primary education may be contrasted with some of the views of Richard Rodriguez, author of *Hunger of Memory* and a critic of both affirmative action and bilingual programs. Rodriguez says, "It is essential that parents and teachers share the same goals for a student."[26] He advocates that literacy programs be made available to persons of all ages. He asserts that cultural minority children need "what any child needs — access to a good school, a school that is safe and quiet, a school with teachers who have a sense of profession, a school where teachers have the time to devote to individual students."

INFORMATION NEEDS RELATED TO VOCATIONS

In addition to the need for good schools, immigrant and minority youth have an urgent need for several types of information related to vocations. Peggy Rubens discusses some of the types of vocational information needed by these young people, including information which will help them to cope with periods of unemployment.[27] Inservice needs of vocational education teachers are listed by Rubens. Public librarians may wish to examine these inservice needs of vocational education teachers and think of the implications for programs which could be provided for potential employers of the youth. Activities for involving parents are suggested by Rubens also; these activities have many implications for school libraries.

Rubens says that immigrant and minority youth have difficulties similar to those of majority youth from low socioeconomic status backgrounds.[28] Educational issues that are of vital importance for immigrant and minority youth are influenced by attitudes and roles: those of "teachers, teacher organizations, teacher training organizations, and school administrators.[29] In addition, attitudes within the family and community can either enhance or detract from the roles youth play. Factors which are important concerning the development of immigrant and minority youth are "language-instruction underachievement, individual learning styles, curriculum, tests, the organization and procedure of schools, and the training of teachers and administrators."[30]

Vocational Education for Immigrant and Minority Youth does not directly mention library materials, but it does mention the information needs of immigrant and minority youth and those of their teachers and their families. Guidelines for the types of materials needed are implied by the information needs specified.

To prepare youth for work, information is needed about:

1. Competencies, behaviors, and attitudes valued in the workplace.
2. Educational and training choices and their implications for occupations.
3. The labor market, detailing the actual qualifications of those who hold the jobs.
4. Ways to acquire a variety of work experiences.
5. Ways to seek jobs, including the use of placement services and employment agencies.

Rubens relays the suggestion of several writers on vocational education that in a time of high unemployment youth should be provided with additional information, such as:

1. Ways to cope with unemployment.
2. Possibilities of entering youth programs sponsored by the government.
3. Acceptance of jobs below the levels expected.
4. Ways to become self-employed.

5. Activities in the community, which may be unpaid, but are useful for gaining experience.
6. Ways to make positive use of leisure time.

Vocational education teachers have needs. Rubens says some of their inservice training needs may include the following:[31]

1. Preparation for working with racial and ethnic groups.
2. Information about dialect speech.
3. Instruction in a foreign language.
4. Seminars on racism, sexism, and other forms of discrimination.
5. Programs to help overcome apathy and renew motivation.
6. Multicultural education preparation.
7. Instruction about various cultures.

Frequently, parents need encouragement to become more involved with their childrens' learning. Rubens points out that sometimes parents with orthodox religious views are more likely than others to fear or reject contacts with schools. Some suggestions for gaining parent participation are offered by Rubens. Each suggestion has some implications for materials which would be useful to implement it or materials which would be needed as a result of an activity. Suggestions include:

1. Arranging for adult language or other classes to meet at a school.
2. "Communicating with the parents of immigrant or minority students in their native language."
3. Sending written progress reports to parents about the academic work of children.
4. School personnel visiting homes of immigrant and minority youth to report progress of problems and to encourage the parents to visit the school.
5. "Appointing cultural liaison teachers to make parents aware of the aims of the schools and to facilitate feedback from parents."
6. "Organizing parent mutual support groups and educating the parent as educators."
7. Scheduling more school visit meetings at times which are convenient for parents.
8. Providing explanations to parents about occupational opportunities.

Rubens says that the women among minority and immigrant young people may feel a special need for information related to women's

issues such as "autonomy, empowerment, independence and asser-
tion."[33] These young women and older women also may experience
wrenching conflict between the roles and expectations of the new
society as opposed to the old. The best ways to effect changes of attitudes in relatives who may wish to keep her in the fully submissive
"female role" and to learn the multiple roles assigned to women in the
United States may vary from the situation of one young woman to
that of another. For those who may try to do them all, it is suggested
that Afro-American women may provide role models.

Sensitizing counselors to the needs of minority and immigrant
youth and to the attitudes of their parents has implications for librarians. Frequent, friendly communications with counselors by librarians
about the counselors' own needs for information and those of the
young people they serve have great potential for opening new opportunities for service. Counselors can be very helpful in identifying
useful materials.

Authoritative guidelines have been produced by the National Institute of Education for the evaluation and successful selection of instructional materials for career education.[34] These guidelines constitute
Volume I of a two-part study. "The two volumes which comprise this
Educational Products Information Exchange (EPIE) Career Education S*E*T (S election and E valuation T ools) are the result of a
nine-month study. . . . Volume II provides descriptions of some 700
career education materials."

Chapter 2 of the EPIE guidelines is entitled "Racism in Materials:
How to Detect It and How to Counteract Its Effects in the Class-
room."[35] A useful checklist for Reviewing Career Education
Materials for Racist Content may be reproduced. Prepared by a team
of persons under contract from the Council on Interracial Books for
Children. This chapter gives clearly written explanations of the types
of racist content which can be detected in many career-education
materials. Other guidelines are provided about sex-role stereotyping.
Of special interest may be chapter 4, entitled "Producers' Evaluation
Activities: How to Assess Them."[36] The entire chapter is especially
useful for educators and school librarians.

CRITERIA: A SUBJECT AREA APPROACH

An examination of the contemporary values which affirm cultural
diversity as a positive characteristic of the heritage of United States

citizens reveals varied expressions of these values. Selection criteria used to evaluate subject areas and the materials used by children and young people must also reflect these values. Art, a prime expression of values, is also an important subject area for evaluation. A 1980 publication entitled *Multicultural Nonsexist Education: Arts Education in Iowa Schools* (available from the Department of Public Instruction, Educational Equity Section, Grimes State Office Building, Des Moines, Iowa 50319) makes suggestions to aid local curriculum committees in the development and implementation of arts education programs which are multicultural and nonsexist.[37] Goals for students include: (1) "develop positive and realistic self concepts"; (2) "understand that both sexes and diverse racial / cultural groups have made valuable contributions to the heritage of the United States"; (3) "understand that all persons . . . have common needs, feelings and problems, while at the same time stimulating their appreciation for the uniqueness of each individual and cultural group"; and (4) "develop positive interpersonal and intergroup communication techniques as well as a motivation to play an active role in the solution of societal conflicts." Two or more objectives are suggested after each expanded goal statement.

In addition to goals and objectives, the Iowa Arts Education pamphlet provides a self-evaluation checklist for:[38] (1) curriculum structure; (3)instructional materials; and (4) teaching strategies. Following the self-evaluation checklist is a bibliography of resource materials.

The checklist for instructional materials concerns whether: (1) the written content is multicultural and nonsexist; (2) illustrations, including bulletin boards, reflect aesthetic contributions and viewpoints of all the society; (3) materials are free of ethnocentric or sexist language patterns; (4) audiovisual materials reflect contributions and viewpoints of all the society; (5) works chosen for study and / or performance come from a diverse group of artists . . . and performers; (6) the aforementioned works reflect a fair balance of aesthetic contributions and viewpoints; and (7) multicultural, nonsexist criteria have been incorporated into the selection process for arts materials at the district level. These criteria are concerned with fairness and diversity of materials related to the arts and in their use for educational purposes.

A different approach is taken in an article by Guy Bensusan which indicates a dynamic diversity in the Mexican American art emerging as an expression of sociopolitical concern in the 1960s, at the time of the Chicano revolution.[39] Many antecedent influences from before the 1960s are described.

Bensusan advocates a holistic approach to the evaluation of Mexican American art.[40] He says, "Since so much of the art is extremely subjective and projective in its insistent concentration on the Mexican American experience, it should be placed in its multicultural and multidisciplinary context."

Bensusan concludes his article with a "Proposed Outline for Context-Oriented Study" or Mexican American art accompanied by "Sources for Study." The outline can serve as a useful guideline for organizing printed and audiovisual materials for the study of Mexican American art. Jacinto Quirarte, dean of the College of Fine Arts of the University of Texas at San Antonio, is preparing packets which include bibliographies, syllabi, and slides for courses in Chicano art.[41]

In the *Sourcebook of Hispanic Culture in the United States*, Catherine E. Wall provides a chapter entitled "Art" in the section of the book about continental Puerto Ricans. Her essay and annotated bibliography are informative and indicative of current trends.[42]

These two sources, one from Iowa and the other related to the art of Hispanic cultural minorities, illustrate two valid and complementary approaches to guidance for the selection of materials: (1) general guidance within a subject area, and (2) culturally explicit guidance. Both are needed.

DETECTION OF CULTURAL FAIRNESS BY CHILDREN AND YOUNG PEOPLE

Robert C. Small, Jr., says students should learn to recognize and resist bias in children's and young adults' literature.[43] In many instances, Small says, authors have been treated as if they were perfect. Small claims, "Bias is nearly as prevalent in classics as it is in 'potboilers.'"

The issue of cultural fairness from a Mexican American perspective is discussed by Oscar Uribe, Jr., Tamara Altman, and James Vasquez.[44] The four criteria which they believe to be useful for analyses from an ethnic perspective are:

1. *validity of information*, which implies the need to check how facts are organized as well as for errors in fact;
2. *unity of information*, which indicates the need to provide viewpoints from all groups concerning a given historical event and important contributions from various cultural groups;

3. *balance*, which implies the need to inspect for representation of various social strata and the contributions of subgroups, such as women, youth, the elderly, and intellectuals, as well as for equitable consideration of cultures; and

4. *realism*, which indicates the need for portrayal of many types (including various body and skin types) of individuals and personalities within a culture who share many things in common but who can at the same time be perceived as existing and functioning as normal individual human beings.

Stilted translations should be avoided. Uribe, Altman, and Vasquez conclude that language, tone, and illustrations in textbooks and stories should assist Mexican American children to feel proud both of being Americans and of their cultural heritage.[45] At the same time, other children should be able to acquire additional knowledge and appreciation of Mexican American culture. Helen W. Painter discusses guidelines for translations. According to her criteria, the complete ideas of the original should be encompassed in the transcript, and the style and manner of writing should reflect the character of the original work.[46]

The issue of cultural fairness from a Chinese perspective is discussed by Shirley Sun, Tamara Altman, and James Vasquez.[47] They testify that Chinese Americans, even of second, third, and fourth generations removed from immigrant status, have been set apart from other Americans because of cultural and physical differences. Indicative is the frequency with which Asian Americans are complimented on how well they speak English.

Two erroneous assumptions about Chinese Americans are "the success myth" and "the proud Chinese myth," both of which imply that no problems exist despite many years of discrimination. Many Chinese American born in the United States have suffered identity conflicts, in some cases forsaking language and cultural activities of their parents.

Omission of the role of their forefathers from historical materials about the United States has contributed to the conflicts coupled with lack of knowledge of their own cultural history. Sun, Altman, and Vasquez deplore the slowness of the addition of the Asian-American contributions to the historical accounts of the United States and the tendency to add the information as separate units rather than integrating it into the historical chronology.

As with the materials concerning Mexican Americans, Sun, Altman, and Vasquez advocate the criterion of *validity of information*. This means in addition to correct facts avoiding stereotypes perpetuated by the "successful" and "proud" Chinese myths and those which relate to "behavior and physical characteristics as clever, loyal, law-abiding, sneaky, hardworking, have short, squat *bodies* and buck teeth." Stereotypical occupations, e.g., "laundryman" and "accountant," or sex roles, e.g., "exotic women" or "studious men," should be avoided.[48]

The criterion of *unity of information* as discussed by Sun, Altman, and Vasquez implies the need to ascertain if the complete range of events concerning Chinese Americans is presented in historical materials, including ethnic group contributions where appropriate and meaningful. It implies also the presentation of group behavior in realistic terms in accordance with the circumstances of the times, e.g., the congregating of Chinese Americans to create Chinatowns in large cities not solely because the Chinese Americans wanted to be together but because they had been forced to move out of many small towns. In addition, materials should not include discussions of former customs "e.g., foot-binding in ancient China or weaving the hair in queues," in a way that leads to the erroneous impression that these are contemporary practices.

For the criterion of *balance*, various social class values within ethnic groups should be shown. One set of values should not be emphasized so strongly that other values are made to appear inferior. Sun, Altman, and Vasquez comment that things which appear "different" in the context of one culture may be effective within another culture. Again, a range of social and occupational activities should be shown with contributions of various individuals and subgroups included. Positive cultural characteristics of Chinese Americans should be shown as well as individual differences among them. Descriptions of Chinese and China from only American perspectives as well as condescending compliments should be avoided.

The criterion of *realism* necessitates watching for the use of correct facts presented in inappropriate contexts so as to give unrealistic impressions. One subculture of Chinese Americans should not be presented as if that way of existence were typical of all Chinese Americans. Inaccurate impressions to be avoided can come from literal translations which imply Chinese use of flowery languge and excessively polite manners, or from descriptions of Chinatown which present it as a glamorous tourist attraction.

Small suggests that it is preferable not to take a didactic approach when helping children to learn about stereotypes.[49] He says that children should be questioned about the characters and encouraged to arrive at their own conclusions. Each work of literature can be approached with such questions as, "Is your mother like that? Is Susan like that? Am I like that? Are you like that?" followed by questions which explore the answer, "How is your mother like the character in the story? List the ways they are alike. How are they different?" Through such explanations, eventually children and young adults can learn to recognize stereotypes and discount their influence.[50]

Although the approach advocated by Small may be useful for learning to contend with biased generalizations concerning personality and characterization, cultural traits, and omissions or distortions of facts, the reader may need added approaches for discerning which facts and characterizations are true-to-life. These additional approaches present opportunities for children and young adults to learn how to check historical presentations for verification of facts and for indications of omissions. Consultation of primary materials as well as studies in the field of social psychology may provide added insights concerning cultural attributes of various groups, so that librarians, teachers, and parents can assist children and young people to verify knowledge and fictional portrayals that are historically and culturally valid.

Adults as well as youth who examine materials for cultural fairness may find it useful to write, as well as to state orally, the ways in which they perceive the contents of materials. Although the authors advocate that facts be checked in reference materials, care must be taken concerning the materials which are used to check for correct information. Textbooks as well as many trade books in libraries may not be reliable sources to use in checking for accurate and comprehensive information in high school textbooks.

An example of the unreliability of information is shown by a study reported from the Council on Interracial Books for Children.[51] In a study coordinated and prepared by Nancy Anderson and Rochelle Beck, a panel of fifteen reviewers knowledgeable about Central America analyzed seventy-one books, including thirty-one high school history texts. A summary of their findings reveals:

1. Central America is shown as unimportant in many books by being (a) omitted entirely in many commonly used history, world geography, and "cultures" books (some books about Latin America omit Central America or do not name the individual countries within the region); (b) given fewer pages than those allocated to other land masses; and (c) referred to as a bridge between North and South America with no description of the nations or peoples included.
2. Racial and ethnic stereotypes can be found in most of the books.
3. Readers of the books are led to the erroneous conclusions that the major causes of underdevelopment and poverty may be attributed to climate, geography, and the shortcomings of Central Americans. Exploitation is seldom mentioned. The history of social and economic structures within each country is not provided. The impact of external economic interests, e.g., the United Fruit Company, is not explained or is erroneously presented.
4. Many books report only those historical facts which relate the economic concerns or strategic interests of the United States.
5. The role of the United States in many Central American countries is erroneously portrayed as that of a helper rather than that of an intervener.
6. Exotic events are emphasized instead of significant achievements. A Eurocentric view of Central American people is provided. Names of specific individuals are not provided.
7. Distorted images of either tranquility or political instability are provided, with no information about contemporary politics or historical contexts.

CULTURAL VALIDITY AND ADULT GUIDANCE

How can the adults who guide children and young people know if the materials available are trustworthy and culturally valid? It is perplexing not to be able to have confidence that all or even most of the contents of available textbooks and library books are valid. Some advice about a process which could help with the effort to acquire culturally valid materials is available from the State of Delaware. The Delaware State Department of Public Instruction is concerned with the uses of materials as well as with the selection of materials for instructional purposes. "Guidelines for Local District Application" is part of a series of guidelines provided, and local district personnel are advised to establish temporary advisory committees when a representative view-point is needed or when additional selection criteria need to be recommended; to involve classroom teachers and instructional personnel in selection of all instructional materials; to provide inservice programs and training sessions for teachers who will use newly acquired materials; to use materials which are considered controversial on a pilot basis until evaluation can be made of their effect prior to widespread use and until study of these materials can be accomplished and to undertake periodic reviews of controversial materials by representative committees of teachers, administrators, students, and interested community persons to provide understanding and support for objectivity in instructional programs.[52]

The Delaware publication provides guidelines entitled "Basic Principles for Minimizing Sexual and Other Biases in the Instructional Program."[53] Examples of the types of information provided are shown below. These guidelines advocate that the instructional staff:

1. Explain how historical events and conditions have been interpreted to the disadvantage of minority groups and women by
   a. negating "myths" which misrepresent or show inaccuracies;
   b. insisting on accuracy or openly stated judgments about the portrayal of historical "heroes"; and
   c. explaining past historical developments which were based on values inconsistent with those usually associated with the political system of the United States.
2. Show present forces and conditions which are disadvantageous for minority groups or for women by
   a. describing conditions of urban as well as rural suburban environments;
   b. showing problems and conditions found at all levels and classes of society;
   c. presenting recent research-based findings;
   d. opposing racism, sexism, and prejudice;
   e. using the scholarly work of minorities and females; and
   f. including minority and female works in bibliographies of printed and audiovisual materials.

These guidelines for persons who provide learning activities for the young are important for those who would provide leadership in the selection and use of instructional materials. Several of the guidelines carry with them the implication that selection of unbiased sources of information and accurately focused information sources is only a portion of the work that needs to be accomplished on behalf of young users of information.

The importance of the development of attitudes, knowledge, skills, and appropriate learning strategies is emphasized in the Delaware guidelines. Access to well-selected information sources is a beginning; new understandings are provided through the activities developed with the information sources. Clearly, several of the Delaware guidelines provide useful ideas to incorporate in locally developed written criteria for the selection and use of materials.

Several types of guidelines are provided by the Division of Elementary and Secondary Education in South Dakota. The "General Guidelines" emphasize the importance of the contemporary realism being reflected in the roles of men, women, and minorities.[54] Typical items in "General Guidelines" advocate that instructional materials should show:

1. "the character, temperament, and traits of males and females of all ages, races, and ethnic backgrounds",
2. members of each sex in attire appropriate to their activities and in accordance with standards of dress which exist; and
3. proportionally historic and current achievements of persons representative of the sex and minority representation in the United States' population — including materials about, and written or composed by, women and minorities.

Following the general guidelines are problems related to the guidelines plus possible solutions. Examination of these problems and solutions can be helpful for persons who wish to improve their ability to discern what materials reflect about the varieties of living conditions and aspirations of individuals in the United States.

A sample checklist accompanied by guidelines is provided to use in examining instructional materials for cultural and racial diversity. The guidelines indicate that users of the checklist should exercise personal judgments about the appropriateness of a given guideline.

The criteria in the checklist are useful, because they include both items concerned with adverse reflections on cultural and racial diversity in materials and items about accurate portrayal of roles. The checklist provides places for the user to indicate page references and comments.

The adverse reflections are concerned with references in materials which: (1) demean, stereotype, or patronize; (2) make adverse judgments about different customs or life styles; or (3) do not show fair proportions of diverse ethnic groups in text or illustrations. The criteria about accurate portrayal of roles reflect the concerns of the "General Guidelines." Each criterion is discussed for the evaluators.

In addition, there is a rating scale for audiovisual materials to screen for racial bias. Consideration is given to blacks, Chicanos, American Indian, Asians, Anglos, and others. The items to be rated correspond to the items on the checklist designed to be used with written materials.

To assist schools, a school self-evaluation scale is provided for use concerning curriculum, community, school board, administration, teachers, students, and guidance.[55] Examples of items by category are:

Curriculum — "When ideal materials cannot be found, are teachers trained to detect and to guide their students to detect both overt and subtle manifestations of racism?"

Community — "Does the LEA maintain a listing of minority resource people and agencies who are available to come into the school and work directly with teachers and students?"

School board — "Do they represent all classes and races in the community?"

Administration — "Are women and minorities invited to address assembly and graduation ceremonies?"

Teachers — "Does the LEA provide its staff with inservice on the differential discipline expectations of different minority groups?"

Students — "Is there evidence that minority students discuss problems with the teaching staff and that the teaching staff attempts to help on these problems?"

The questions in the guidance category were about sex-role stereotyping. The rating scale provides for indicating one of four responses: yes, always; sometimes; rarely; and no, never.

Individual writers may provide guidelines which are useful for the selectors of materials to be used by young people. One of them is Frank Chin, a Chinese American playwright and one of the editors of *Aiiieeeee! An Anthology of Asian-American Writers*.

Frank Chin deplores the cultural losses of contemporary Asian Americans and largely blames white writers in the United States.[56]

He writes, "Memory of the links between the early Chinese and Japanese Americans' folk, popular and mythic images of themselves and today's Asian America is pretty well gone." He attributes this loss to "missionary science fiction from Charlie Chan to Pearl Buck to the ugly little *The Five Chinese Brothers*." Chin cites consistent misrepresentation of Asian as well as Asian-American history and culture by the dominant group in the United States.

Chin values the works of Taro Yashima and Lawrence Yep as those that show "the literary sensibility, language and vision of the universe Asian and Asian American." Chin asserts that "People are pushing 'interaction with the dominant group' as a criterion for children's books on yellows and badmouthing books that show Asian Americans socializing exclusively with their own. We're teaching kids to value white society above their own with that 'interaction with the dominant culture' line."

Although several lists of criteria suggest that the background of authors and illustrators should be examined to ascertain their qualifications for the contributions they make to children's materials, few guidelines suggest examining children's and young peoples' collections for the quantity and quality of materials which show members of ethnic or cultural groups "socializing exclusively with their own." Chin says that portrayal of interaction of a minority group with the dominant group should not be considered as the criterion of a good book. This is a guideline more important than many which are commonly provided—both for the young of the group depicted, whereby their imaginations are stimulated and the sense of their own people instilled, and for the young of other groups, who may more clearly learn of the common human concerns, but varied customs, of others.

Another source of guidelines is the State Department of Education in Maryland. The Maryland *Guidelines* are divided into three sections: general criteria, criteria for factual materials, and criteria for imaginative materials.[57] Under *general criteria*, the potential selectors are told that:

1. Presentation of a character who displays less than admirable behavior should be analyzed to ascertain that there is reason and motivation for the behavior other than that the character is the member of a minority group.
2. Materials should enable a minority child to identify with individuals and groups, and develop respect for others who differ from

her / him. In order to avoid materials which may potentially offend another individual, the selector is advised to ask how he or she as a person from the minority group discussed in the material would feel about using the material being evaluated. In addition, the evaluator should question what attitude a white person might form through use of the material.

3. Positive aspects of contemporary life, e.g., strengths and positive values ghetto residents use to cope with the environment, can be conveyed to to children.

A sample of items among *criteria for factual materials* states:

1. Include controversial and unpleasant matters, e.g., frank treatments of political, economic and social evils, rather than defending, minimizing, or ignoring them.
2. Include works which reflect authoritative and comprehensive treatments based on current research.
3. Include materials on racial and minority group participation in all disciplines and facets of American life, historically as well as currently.
4. Seek print and nonprint materials which reflect cultural pluralism and show diverse factors which affect groups and thereby eliminate stereotyping.

Similar advice is provided about imaginative materials, e.g., novels, stories, poetry, and nonfactual films. Imaginative materials should:

1. contain emotional interpretations which can withstand critical review;
2. deemphasize words which may strain relations between individuals or groups; and
3. Include works directed toward adults when selected for users in secondary schools.[58]

Those who developed the Maryland *Guidelines* consider them to be general and equally applicable to materials concerning any minority group. It is evident that the developers of these criteria kept constantly before them the goal of selecting materials to promote healthy self-concepts of minority children and to provide them with information and creative material to promote their intellectual and emotional growth.

So, as this chapter has demonstrated, there are various types of guidelines for educators and librarians: guidelines for the selection of specific types of materials, e.g., bilingual and vocational materials; and general guidelines concerning processes to use in selecting materials or procedures to use to insure that knowledgeable persons are involved in selection procedures. Several varieties of agencies exist to provide information and referral services.

PROMISE OF THE FUTURE: THE YOUNG CHILD

The growth and development of young children is the concern of both families and communities. In an address on "The American Family 1978: Human Values and Public Policy," Irving M. Levine[59] advocated a "social conservation approach" to family and community coping wherein: (1) individuals may relate positively to their group identity; (2) the existing natural and informal systems of family, neighborhood, work, religion, and ethnic group form a basis for provision of services; (3) programs are structured to offer choices of forms of help available in various environments — ethnic, religious, social, and economic; and (4) professional and technical assistance is meshed with experience and common sense of the persons within the various communities.

Vegetable Soup: Parent-Teacher Guide, an undated publication — issued after May of 1975 — available from the University of the State of New York, the State Education Department, Bureau of Mass Communications, Albany, New York 12234, may be useful for educators and librarians who work with young children. *Vegetable Soup* is concerned with human-relations concepts to be learned by young children. Teaching techniques and learning objectives are specified.

Typical "Attitudinal and Behavioral Objectives" addressed are:

1. to recognize differences in other persons and to consider them in a positive light;
2. to include the "left-out" child or children in the "in" group;
3. to recognize and respect the rights and privileges of others;
4. to recognize the interdependence of all people;
5. to motivate children to think about themselves and others and their influences upon one another;
6. to consider and respect the feelings of others;

7. to learn that nonacceptance of others does harm to both the name-caller and the one who is verbally attacked; and

8. to learn about children of different races and socioeconomic backgrounds.[60]

Guidelines of value for programming may also include those provided by Marguerite Baechtold and Eleanor Ruth McKinney in their book *Library Service for Families*[61] and research findings reported by Frances Smardo and Velma Schmidt in their article in the *Southeastern Librarian* (Summer 1984) entitled "Using Books to Help Teachers and Children Develop Multicultural Awareness."[62] Ideas for programs about cultural diversity are provided by Melinda Greenblatt's article "Expanding Children's Programming in School and Public Libraries," which appeared in the October 1979 issue of the *Wilson Library Bulletin.*[63]

These guidelines relate to programming or use of materials rather than their selection. With very young children, availability of materials alone is not enough; they must be shared by an adult. It is the interests, the values, and the enthusiasms of the adults that influence children in homes, schools, and libraries. These values and enthusiasms are projected in the activities which stimulate children's interests and their acquisition of attitudes and knowledge. The types of materials needed vary with programming objectives and activities. Since the school is a microcosm of society, the child can find bias within the general culture at an early age. Geraldine L. Wilson reports that "racism and sexism still pervade the toy market."[64] She says that Asian, Latino, Native American and African American dolls are manufactured by a black-owned doll company. If the dolls are not available in a neighborhood store, the address of the company in Shindana Toys, P.O. Box 71466, 6107 S. Central Avenue, Los Angeles, Calif. 90001.

Harry W. Sartain concludes from a review of research about family contributions to reading attainment that more functional knowledge for many children is gained from the home and the community than from the school. In addition to parents, siblings, aunts, uncles, and grandparents can provide cultural and learning experiences supportive of the child.[65] Anthropologist Henry G. Burger says variables in a school's subculture — the sociological environment, the teaching methods, the subjects taught, and the people or things with whom a student identifies — need to be linked with a student's out-of-school culture so that the variables become mutually reinforcing.[66]

An area in which Burger sees that more could be done is the field of academic games. He says, "Social science courses presenting the development of the United States should consider the pioneers from the several ethnic groups, their explorers and soldiers. Courses might recreate events from which these ethnic minorities emigrated. Curricula in literature should include readings about and by members of that ethnic group. Studies in art and music should consider all types of aesthetics of the minority groups. Painting and orchestra classes should offer these various styles, as should dancing, an activity generally more institutionalized in the non-Anglo cultures of the world than among the Anglos. (It would fit the children's sex roles, of course, not necessarily being of mixed-sex couples as in the nuclear Anglo style.)"[67] Incorporation of minority art forms into arts and crafts courses is advocated. In home economics courses, types of foods and facilities for cooking should be considered. In order to treat cultural heritages as integral and valuable rather than as extraordinary, Burger advocates that advisory committees be formed of minority adults.

Burger advocates that various shades of opinion be included in library materials — those of the middle class and also the separatists among a minority. Burger says the issues these materials "raise are real issues that cannot be ignored by the school designed to be involved with its community."[68] Many of the ideas advocated by Burger concerning curricula and materials are applicable to the programming activities of public libraries which are designed for children and young adults.

When developing a collection of children's books from other countries and in other languages, there is a need to identify sources of these materials, which, in some instances, may be difficult to find. The Information Center on Children's Cultures, a service of the United States Committee for UNICEF, has a list entitled "Sources of Children's Books from Other Countries and in Other Languages," which is frequently revised.[69] Excerpts from the most recent (1982) revision include the following information. The list is neither selective nor all-inclusive.

Children's books from other countries can be used very successfully in many international or intercultural programs. Although some of these books are cheaply produced paperbacks, they are often interesting and attractive, and children respond very quickly to the idea that they are handling something authentic. Many are in English (e.g., those from India and parts of Africa) as well as in other languages. Many can prove helpful in getting children to identify with the cultural heritage from which their families come. Some of the companies listed here sell materials written in other languages but published in the U.S.

Any school, library or individual needing help in selecting lists of children's materials in languages which are not widely spoken or understood in the U.S. (e.g., Swahili, Portuguese, Hindi) should write to the Information Center on Children's Cultures, U.S. Committee for UNICEF, 331 East 38th St., New York, N.Y. 10016. Please indicate what the specific need is, age level, etc. Be sure to enclose a *legal-size, stamped, self-addressed envelope.*

Lucretia M. Harrison provides a list of "Do's and Don't's of Collecting Foreign Children's Books," as well as advice about building a minicollection.[70] Marie Zielinska and Irena Bell provide additional valuable advice in their article "Selection and Acquisition of Library Materials in Languages Other than English: Some Guidelines for Public Libraries," in *Collection Building.*[71]

Useful lists of additional resource organizations can be made by searching the ERIC documents, e.g., *Guide to Resource Organizations for Minority Language Groups. Resources in Bilingual Education* (ED 203 693) lists 242 organizations.

IMPLICATIONS FOR IMPROVED SERVICES

Some implications concerning the use of selection guidelines are:

1. Teachers and librarians need to continue their efforts to learn about the cultures of the community they serve and the cultures that exist outside their immediate communities.
2. Teachers and librarians should become skilled in locating materials and applying various types of selection criteria to them.
3. Teachers and librarians need to instruct children and young people how to use selection criteria with materials.
4. Issues of censorship must be addressed by professional personnel as well as children and youth. Obviously, indications of racism and stereotypes are prevalent in materials; not all existing materials

identified as having omissions or errors of fact will be removed as sources of information in either public schools or libraries. Analyses and discussions between youth and adults about these matters are important forerunners to weeding out and replacing materials that, while not totally desirable, are not blatantly destructive and harmful.

5. Involvement of community persons and family members in selection procedures and programming activities is advisable.

6. Development by librarians and teachers of personal networks of resources, both human and material, aids in providing the best possible service to all.

CONTACTING FAMILIAR PROFESSIONAL ORGANIZATIONS

Contacts with the primary professional organizations of teachers and librarians can provide new sources of information. For instance, in 1980 the National Education Association issued a *Selected and Annotated Bibliography on Teaching Refugee Children*.[72] This bibliography is concerned with Indochinese, Haitian, and Cuban refugees. The bibliography informs teachers of non-English-speaking refugee children about "(1) some of the materials that are available to help them teach English to these children, and (2) sources of information on Teaching Refugee Children." The American Library Association has Ethnic Materials Information Exchange Round Table. Membership is $5.00, whether or not a person is a member of the American Library Association. Members receive copies of the *EMIE Bulletin*. A recent program of the Ethnic Materials Information Exchange Round Table concerned contacts with alternative publishers to locate additional publications. Several subcommittees of the American Library Association are working on, or have recently worked on, guidelines or other publications related to topics of this book. An example of work now in progress includes the Proposed Reference and Adult Services Divisions "Guidelines for Library Services to Hispanics," Committee on Service to the Spanish Speaking, under Nathan A. Josel, chairperson.[73] A book about a core collection of materials related to needs of Spanish-speaking persons, scheduled to be published within the next two years, has been developed by the Reference and Adult Services Division of the American Library Association. Materials useful for children and young adults are included in this forthcoming publication.

GUIDELINES RELATED TO EFFECTIVENESS

Both specialized lists and general lists exist which relate to the users of materials and their effects on users. Theodore Andersson's *A Guide to Family Reading in Two Languages: The Preschool Years* includes a list which can be useful for parents who wish to raise bilingual and biliterate children.[74] It contains twenty suggestions about speaking, reading, listening, writing, and other activities, such as, playing games and visiting community cultural centers. For public librarians who work with preschool children, the suggestions can be adapted for parents of children who speak only English as well as for bilingual or multilingual parents. The suggestions provide a positive and active approach to parenting and the transmittal of cultural values to children.

Max Rosenberg's "Criteria for Evaluating the Treatment of Minority Groups and Women in Textbooks and Other Learning Materials," which appeared originally in *Educational Leadership* 31 (November 1973): 108-9, provides guidelines which are frequently reprinted. They can be found in Banks's *Teaching Strategies for Ethnic Studies.*[75] Examples of the twenty criteria are:

15. Supply an accurate and sound balance in the matter of historical perspective, making it perfectly clear that all racial, religious and ethnic groups have mixed heritages which can well serve as sources of group pride and group humility.
17. Clarify the true contemporary forces and conditions which at present operate to the disadvantage of women and minority groups.[76]

Banks has also provided a reprint of the "Multiethnic Education Program Evaluation Checklist." This checklist originally appeared in *Curriculum Guidelines for Multiethnic Education*, by James A. Banks, Carlos E. Cortés, Geneva Gay, Ricardo L. Garcia, and Anna S. Ochoa (Washington, D.C.: National Council for the Social Studies, 1976); 42-48. Ratings extend across a four-category scale from a designation of "Strongly" to "Hardly at All." Examples of items include: "13.4. Does content related to ethnic groups extend beyond special units, courses, occasions, and holidays?" and "17.0. Does the curriculum help students to view and interpret events, situations, and conflict from diverse ethnic perspectives and points of view?"[77]

Guidelines exist for analyzing the effectiveness of presentations presented on instructional television, e.g., *Guidelines for Avoiding Biases and Stereotypes in Instructional Television.*[78] Prepared for the Production of the Essential Learning Skills Television Project Series THINK-ABOUT. Three categories are the concern of these guidelines: the extent of representation of ethnic groups, quality control, and curriculum content. Four major criteria are related to the quality control category: balance, authenticity, potency, and universality. The guideline concerning the extent of representation of ethnic groups and the quality control categories could be adapted to be used with commercial television programs. The data which young persons might gather from analyzing the same program presentations could provide useful information on which to base discussions about bias and stereotypes.

Effective work with others, in education, librarianship, and related fields, begins and ends with the efforts of individuals. There is no substitute for personal contacts developed with individuals and agencies and communication, over time, about their recent activities and programming efforts. A lively account of public library services to many immigrants in the United States is provided in French by Marie-Noëlle Icardo, conservateur à la bibliothèque municipale et interuniversitaire de Clermont-Ferrand.[79] Her article "Immigrés et bibliothèques aux États-Unis" appears in *Bulletin des bibliothèque de France.* The author observed services in visits to twenty-two libraries located in New York; New Orleans; Tucson, Arizona; San Francisco and Oakland, California; and New Richmond, Wisconsin. Her observations include comments on the bilingual abilities, or lack thereof, in the libraries visited; and cooperative efforts of librarians, such as, the California Ethnic Services Task Force, which had produced a bibliography entitled "Asian Languages Library Materials: Chinese, Philippino, Vietnamese Bibliographies." Books for children are included for each of the languages. Icardo reports the collaboration between the New Richmond Public Library and the College of Education at Indianhead in Wisconsin. Vietnamese materials from the college are deposited in the municipal library because it is nearer to the homes of users. A seminar is provided to aid Vietnamese users with information about vocational and financial matters. Materials produced in Vietnamese and English by the University of Wisconsin concerning household management and family planning are made available in the public library, and this is typical of some of the assistance provided. Icardo describes a story-hour session at the Latin American Center in Oakland, California. She says a Cuban American librarian tells stories in Spanish to children, one-third of whom were born in Mexico. In addition, Icardo noted that English-speaking children were listening to the stories in Spanish also as a part of the effort of their instructors to have children become acquainted with a language and a culture different from their own.

Hispanic and Asian-Pacific children are in our schools; more of them and their families will be living in a great variety of American communities. They are here to stay. Further, they will play important roles in running our country tomorrow. Among other things, they will vote to support, or not to support, libraries in schools, in colleges and in communities. It behooves librarians — spurred on, perhaps even inspired by, this book — to obtain and use the increasing numbers and types of guidelines that are sure to come, suggesting services, giving help with selection and use of materials, and outlining ways to assess the effects of these materials — for the short and the long term. Opportunities exist for an enormous social contribution as well as personal satisfaction and professional growth.

NOTES

PART 1

Chapter 1.
Selection of Materials in the Context of Library Services

1. Sylva N. Manoogian, "The Importance of Ethnic Collections in Libraries," in *Ethnic Collections in Libraries*, ed. E. J. Josey and Marva L. Deloach (New York: Neal Schuman Publishers, 1983), 6.

2. Ibid.

3. National Commission on Excellence in Education. *A Nation at Risk: the Imperative for Educational Reform.* Washington, D.C.: U.S. Government Printing Office, 1984.

4. U.S. Department of Education. *Alliance for Excellence: Librarians Respond to a Nation at Risk.* Washington, D.C.: U.S. Government Printing Office, 1984.

5. "November 18, 1979: General Session III — Presentation of Resolutions," in *Information for the 1980's: Final Report of The White House Conference on Library and Information Services, 1979* (Washington, D.C.: U.S. Government Printing Office, 1980), 243.

6. National Council of Teachers of English. Resolution at Annual Conference. *School Library Journal*, 7 (March 1985): 81–82.

7. "Governing Society: Major R. Owens," in *Information for the 1980's*, 178.

8. Thomas Childers, *The Information-Poor in America* (Metuchen, N.J.: Scarecrow Press, 1975), 90–91.

9. National Commission on Libraries and Information Science. Report of the Task Force on Library and Information Service to Cultural Minorities. Washington, D.C.: U.S. Government Printing Office, 1983.

10. Ibid.

11. "Testimony Submitted by David Cohen," in *Information for the 1980's*, 501.

12. Ernest L. Boyer, "The Test of Growing Student Diversity," *New York Times*, 11 November 1984, sec. 12, 63.

13. A. Harry Passow, "Urban Education for the 1980s: Trends and Issues," *Phi Delta Kappan* 63 (April 1982): 521.

14. Ibid.

15. Ibid., 522.

16. "Testimony Submitted by Thomas C. Battle," in *Information for the 1980's*, 481.

17. Queens Borough Public Library, New Americans Project (single-page informative announcement).

18. Adriana Acauan Tandler, Alan Wagner, and Elizabeth Hsu, *Library Services to Non-English-Speaking Populations, The Queens Model: A Directory of Service Agencies* (New York: Neal Schuman Publishers, 1984), 28–37.

19. Yolanda Cuesta and Patricia Tarin, "Guidelines for Library Service to the Spanish-speaking: A Draft Program for Library Service to 11.3 Million Americans . . . ," *Library Journal* 103 (July 1978): 1350–55.

20. Pennsylvania Department of Education, *Guidelines for Creating Positive Sexual and Racial Images in Educational Materials*, adapted from *Guidelines*, developed by Macmillan Publishing Co., Inc. (New York: Macmillan, 1975), 40, 43.

21. Donald T. Mizokawa and James K. Morishima, "The Education For, By, and Of Asian / Pacific Americans," *Research Review of Equal Education* 3 (Summer 1979): 10–11.

22. James A. Banks, "The Multiethnic Curriculum: Goals and Characteristics," in *Teaching Ethnic Studies: Concepts and Strategies*, ed. James A. Banks (Washington, D.C.: National Council for the Social Studies, 1973), 107.

23. Pamela L. Tiedt and Iris M. Tiedt, *Multicultural Teaching: A Handbook of Activities, Information, and Resources* (Boston: Allyn & Bacon, 1979), 5–6, 7, 11, 12, 15.

24. Yukihisa Suzuki, "Library Services: Education for Librarians and Library Users in a Multi-Lingual Multi-Ethnic Environment," in *Proceedings of IFLA Worldwide Seminar*, May 31–June 5 1976, ed. Ke Hong Park, Dorothy Anderson, and Peter Harvard-Williams (Seoul: Korean Library Association, 1976), 96.

Chapter 2.
Inservice Training / Staff Development

1. Radha Rasmussen and Ivan Kolarik, "Public Library Services to Ethnocultural Minorities in Australia: A State-of-the-Art Survey," *Library Trends* 29 (Fall 1980): 299, citing A. J. Grassby, "Community Relations Means Us All." In Margarita Bowen, ed. *Australia 2000: The Ethnic Impact.* (Armidale, Australia, University of New England Publishing Unit, 1977), 7.

2. Juliana Bayfield, "Children's Library Services for Multicultural Societies in Australia," *International Library Review* 14 (July 1982): 291.

3. Hanna S. Marti and Hans G. Schulte-Albert, "Public Library Services for Immigrants in Sweden," *Canadian Library Journal* 39 (February 1982): 27.

4. Ibid.

5. Ibid., 28.

6. Walter Scherf, "International Youth Library: Achievements and Prospects within a Multicultural Context," *UNESCO Journal of Information Science, Librarianship, and Archives Administration* 1 (January–March 1979): 27.

7. S. Simsova, "The Marginal Man," *Journal of Librarianship* 6 (January 1974): 46–53.

8. Rasmussen and Kolarik, "Public Library Services," 302.

9. Robin Knight with Michael Bosc, Douglas C. Lyons, and Ron Scherer, "American Dream: Alive and Well in the 1980's," *U.S. News & World Report* 97, 10 December 1984, 42.

10. Gary Rubin, "Migration and Mental Health: Implications of Recent Findings," *Migration Today* 9 (Original Pagination 6–12.) Reprint of the Institute on Pluralism and Group Identity, American Jewish Committee, Project on Group Life and Ethnic America, 612 West 57th Street, New York, N.Y. 10022.

11. Frances Haley et al., *Ethnic Studies Handbook for School Librarians* (Arlington, Va.: ERIC Document Reproduction Service, 1978, ED 167 460), 1–30.

12. Edith W. King, *Teaching Ethnic Awareness: Methods and Materials for the Elementary School* (Santa Monica, Calif.: Goodyear, 1980), 76–89.

13. Ibid., 35.

14. Haley, *Ethnic Studies Handbook*, 26–29; King, *Teaching Ethnic Awareness*, 76–77.

15. Muriel Saville-Troike, *A Guide to Culture in the Classroom* (Rosslyn, Va.: National Clearinghouse for Bilingual Education, 1978), 1.

16. King, *Teaching Ethnic Awareness*, 6.

17. Saville-Troike, *A Guide to Culture*, 1.

18. Ibid., 19.

19. James A. Banks, *Teaching Strategies for Ethnic Studies*, 3d ed. (Boston: Allyn & Bacon, 1984), 17–18.

20. Saville-Troike, *A Guide to Culture*, 19–34.

21. Cultural headings are those listed by Saville-Troike; comments are by the authors.

22. Jennifer E. Bahowick, *The Status of School Library Services to Bilingual-Bicultural Programs in Illinois* (Arlington, Va.: ERIC Document Reproduction Service, 1979, ED 179 225), 92.

23. Ibid.

24. Commission for Racial Equality, London (England), *Public Library Services for a Multi-Cultural Society*, rev. ed. (Arlington, Va.: ERIC Document Reproduction Service, 1978, ED 182 356), 8.

25. Ibid.

26. *Manual for Providing Library Services to Indians and Mexican Americans* (Arlington, Va.: ERIC Document Reproduction Service, 1970, ED 047 872), viii.

27. Bayfield, "Children's Library Services," 298.

28. Rasmussen and Kolarik, Public Library Services, 312.

29. Ibid., 305–6.

30. Ibid., 309.

31. Roderick G. Swartz, "Pride in Heritage: One Library's Approach," *Wilson Library Bulletin* 46 (January 1972): 431–35; Dorothy Nyren, "Voices of Brooklyn: Report on a Project Funded by the National Endowment for the Humanities," *Wilson Library Bulletin* 46 (January 1972): 434–45.

32. Swartz, "Pride in Heritage," 434–35.

33. Nyren, "Voices of Brooklyn," 445.

34. Bayfield, "Children's Library Services," 296–97.

35. Marti and Schulte-Albert, "Public Library Services," 31.

36. Haley, *Ethnic Studies Handbook*, 48–49.

37. Bayfield, "Children's Library Services," 297.

PART 2

Introduction

1. Tim Schreiner, "New Hispanic Generation Changing Face of USA," *USA Today*, 14 July 1983, Sec. A.
2. Edwin O. Reischauer, Foreword, in *Becoming Americans*, ed. Tricia Knoll (Portland, Ore.: Coast to Coast Books, 1982), unpaged.
3. Edith W. King, *Teaching Ethnic Awareness: Methods and Materials for the Elementary School* (Santa Monica, Calif.: Goodyear, 1980), 7.

Chapter 3.
Backgrounds of Hispanic Children and Young People in the United States

1. George H. Brown et al., *The Condition of Education for Hispanic Americans* (Washington, D.C.: U.S. Government Printing Office, 1980), 4.
2. Ibid., 2.
3. Schreiner, "New Hispanic Generation," 1A.
4. Brown, *The Condition of Education*, 3.
5. Ibid., 3, 12.
6. Ibid., 3.
7. Ibid., 14.
8. Ibid., 1.
9. Ibid., 3.
10. Schreiner, "New Hispanic Generation," 1A.
11. Ibid., 1A–2A.
12. Ibid., 2A.
13. Brown, *The Condition of Education*, 4.
14. Ibid., xvii.
15. Vincent N. Parrillo, *Strangers to These Shores: Race and Ethnic Relations in the United States* (Boston: Houghton Mifflin, 1980), 422.
16. Ibid., 423–24.
17. Ibid., 424.
18. James A. Banks, *Teaching Strategies for Ethnic Studies*, 2d ed. (Boston: Allyn & Bacon, 1979), 276.
19. George I. Sanchez, Foreword to *Mexican Americans in School: A History of Educational Neglect* (New York: College Entrance Examination Board, 1970), xi.
20. Feliciano Rivera, Introduction to *A Documentary History of the Mexican Americans*, ed. Wayne Moquin with Charles Van Doren (New York: Praeger, 1971), xiii.
21. John H. Burma, *Mexican-Americans in the United States: A Reader* (Cambridge, Mass.: Schenkman, 1970), xiv.
22. Banks, 2d ed. *Teaching Strategies*, 278–79.
23. Ibid., 279.
24. Ibid., 279–80.
25. Charles B. Brussell, *Disadvantaged Mexican American Children and Early Educational Experience* (Austin, Tex.: Southwest Educational Development Corporation, 1968), 10.
26. Rivera, Introduction, xiv.

27. Brussell, *Disadvantaged Mexican American Children*, 11.
28. Burma, *Mexican-Americans*, 11.
29. Ibid.
30. Brussell, *Disadvantaged Mexican American Children*, 11.
31. Ibid., 12.
32. Burma, *Mexican-Americans*, 12.
33. Brussell, *Disadvantaged Mexican American Children*, 12.
34. Ibid., 12-13.
35. Ibid., 13.
36. Burma, *Mexican-Americans*, 14.
37. Ibid.
38. Ibid., 16.
39. Carey McWilliams, *North from Mexico: The Spanish-Speaking People of the United States* (New York: J. B. Lippincott, 1949), 153-56.
40. Ibid., 144-53.
41. Ibid., 160.
42. Ibid., 142-44.
43. Ibid., 161.
44. John H. Burma, *Spanish-Speaking Groups in the United States* (Durham, N.C.: Duke University Press, 1954), 71.
45. Sources for the background readings about Mexican Americans include recommendations of: Banks, *Teaching Strategies*, 2d ed., 132, 294-95, 297-98; Lois Buttlar and Lubomyr R. Wynar, *Building Ethnic Collections: An Annotated Guide for School Media Centers and Public Libraries* (Littleton, Colo.: Libraries Unlimited, 1977), 274, 278, 280, 282-83, 287; David William Foster, ed., *Sourcebook of Hispanic Culture in the United States* (Chicago: American Library Association, 1982), 10, 23, 25, 27, 31, 37, 53, 55, 99.
46. Banks, *Teaching Strategies*, 2d ed., 349.
47. Ibid., 348.
48. Ibid., 347-48.
49. Ibid., 355-56.
50. Ibid., 356.
51. Ibid., 352.
52. Ibid., 350-51.
53. Ibid., 352.
54. Parrillo, *Strangers to These Shores*, 412.
55. Ibid., 416.
56. Ibid., 417.
57. Banks, *Teaching Strategies*, 2d ed., 358.
58. Ibid., 356.
59. Parrillo, *Strangers to These Shores*, 412.
60. Banks, *Teaching Strategies*, 2d ed., 355.
61. Ibid., 356-58.
62. Sources for the background readings about Puerto Rican Americans include recommendations of: Banks, *Teaching Strategies*, 365-66; Diane Herrera, ed., *Puerto Ricans and Other Minority Groups in the Continental United States: An Annotated Bibliography* (Detroit, Mich.: Ethridge, Blaine, Books, 1979), the title as a source; *Interracial Books for Children Bulletin* 14, nos. 1 and 2 (1983): 30; and nos. 3 and 4 (1983): 29.

63. Parrillo, *Strangers to These Shores*, 419.
64. Banks, *Teaching Strategies*, 2d ed., 379–80.
65. James Kelly, "Closing the Golden Door," *Time*, 18 May 1981, 27.
66. Sources for the background readings about Cuban Americans include recommendations of: Banks, *Teaching Strategies*, 2d ed., 394; Wayne Charles Miller, *A Handbook of American Minorities* (New York: New York University Press, 1976), 189; Naomi E. Lindstrom, "Cuban American and Continental Puerto Rican Literature," in Foster, *Sourcebook of Hispanic Culture*, 230.

Chapter 4.
Backgrounds of East Asian Children and Young People in the United States

1. Bureau of the Census, *1980 Census of the Population (Supplementary Reports): Race of the Population by States* (Washington, D.C.: U.S. Government Printing Office, 1980), 13.
2. Knoll, *Becoming Americans*, 7.
3. Ibid., 313.
4. Miller, *A Handbook of American Minorities*, 155.
5. Parrillo, *Strangers to These Shores*, 269.
6. Banks, *Teaching Strategies*, 2d ed., 305.
7. Knoll, *Becoming Americans*, 36, 21.
8. Banks, *Teaching Strategies*, 2d ed., 307.
9. Ibid., 304.
10. Ibid., 309.
11. Sources for the background readings about Chinese Americans include recommendations of: Banks, *Teaching Strategies*, 2d ed., 117; Miller, *A Handbook of American Minorities*, 159, 161.
12. Banks, *Teaching Strategies*, 311.
13. Parrillo, *Strangers to These Shores*, 285.
14. Ibid.
15. Banks, *Teaching Strategies*, 2d ed., 312.
16. Ibid.
17. Parrillo, *Strangers to These Shores*, 286.
18. Ibid., 291.
19. Gene N. Levine and Colbert Rhodes, *The Japanese American Community* (New York: Praeger, 1981), 145.
20. Parrillo, *Strangers to These Shores*, 292.
21. Ibid.
22. Ibid.
23. Sources for the background readings about Japanese Americans include recommendations of: *Focus on Asian Studies* 2 (Winter 1983): 48; Banks, *Teaching Strategies*, 2d ed., 117.
24. Parrillo, *Strangers to These Shores*, 293.
25. Banks, *Teaching Strategies*, 2d ed., 319.
26. Parrillo, *Strangers to These Shores*, 294.
27. Banks, *Teaching Strategies*, 2d ed., 319.
28. Parrillo, *Strangers to These Shores*, 295.

29. Ibid.

30. Ibid., 296.

31. Knoll, *Becoming Americans*, 104.

32. Ibid., 105.

33. Bureau of the Census, *Japanese, Chinese, and Filipinos in the United States: Subject Report* (Washington, D.C.: U.S. Government Printing Office, 1973), 31–45.

34. Knoll, *Becoming Americans*, 108.

35. Ibid., 109.

36. Sources for the background readings about Filipino Americans include recommendations of: Peter Moy, *An Annotated List of Selected Resources for Promoting and Developing an Understanding of Asian Americans*, Bulletin no. 9376 (Madison: Office of Equal Educational Opportunity, Wisconsin Department of Public Instruction, 1978), 28–30; Banks, *Teaching Strategies*, 2d ed., 117–18; Miller, *A Handbook of American Minorities*, 173.

37. Parrillo, *Strangers to These Shores*, 297.

38. Wayne Patterson and Kim Hyung-Chan, *The Koreans in America, 1882–1974* (Minneapolis, Minn.: Lerner Publications, 1977), 34.

39. Knoll, *Becoming Americans*, 120–21.

40. Ibid., 121.

41. Ibid., 123–24.

42. Ibid., 126.

43. Ibid.

44. Ibid., 139.

45. Ibid., 134.

46. Ibid.

47. Ibid., 136.

48. The sources for the background readings about Korean Americans include recommendations of: Moy, *An Annotated List of Selected Resources*, 23; Knoll, *Becoming Americans*, 333.

49. Parrillo, *Strangers to These Shores*, 300.

50. Ibid., 301.

51. Knoll, *Becoming Americans*, 195.

52. Banks, *Teaching Strategies*, 3d ed., 390.

53. Parrillo, *Strangers to These Shores*, 303–7.

54. Sources for the background readings about Vietnamese Americans are the recommendations of: *Focus on Asian Studies* 1 (Fall 1983): 24; Alan B. Henkin and Liem Thanh Nguyen, *Between Two Cultures: The Vietnamese in America* (Saratoga, Calif.: Century Twenty-One Publishing, 1981), 66.

55. Monica Armour, Paula Knudsen, and Jeffrey Meeks, eds. *The Indochinese: New Americans* (Provo, Utah: Center for International and Area Studies, Brigham Young University Publication Services, 1981), 26.

56. Knoll, *Becoming Americans*, 222.

57. Ibid., 313.

58. Sources for the background readings about Laotian Americans include: National Education Association, *Selected and Annotated Bibliography on Teaching Refugee Children: Indochinese, Haitian, Cuban*, (Washington, D.C.: National Education Association, 1980), 11–12; Knoll, *Becoming Americans*, 334–35.

59. Armour, *The Indochinese*, 22–23.

60. Knoll, *Becoming Americans*, 284.

61. Armour, *The Indochinese*, 23.

62. Knoll, *Becoming Americans*, 292.

63. Ibid., 299.

64. Ibid., 290.

65. Ibid., 294.

66. Ibid., 313.

67. Sources for the background readings about Kampuchean Americans include: *Focus on Asian Studies* 3 (Winter 1984): 53; Knoll, *Becoming Americans*, 335.

PART 3

Chapter 5.
Selection of Culturally Relevant Materials:
Guidelines and Related Issues

1. Phyllis J. Van Orden, *The Collection Program in Elementary and Middle Schools: Concepts, Practices and Information Sources* (Littleton, Colo.: Libraries Unlimited, 1982), 38–43.

2. Ibid., 41.

3. Helen Huus, "Evaluation of Children's Literature," in *Insights Into Why and How to Read*, ed. Robert T. Williams (Newark, Del.: International Reading Association, 1976), 23–29.

4. Grace W. Ruth, "Selecting Children's Books to Meet Multicultural Needs." *Catholic Library World* 55 (November 1983): 169–70.

5. James M. Anderson, "Developing Criteria for Evaluating Ethnic Studies Materials." (New York: Institute of Human Relations, June 1974); two pages reprinted from *Audiovisual Instruction* 17 (November 1972): 1.

6. J. D. McAulay, "Evaluation of Textbook Content on Southeast Asia," *The Clearing House* 52 (November 1978): 105.

7. Ibid. 105–106.

8. Charlotte S. Huck, *Children's Literature in the Elementary School*, 3d. rev. ed. (New York: Holt, Rinehart & Winston, 1979), 16–17.

9. Margaret R. Marshall, *An Introduction to the World of Children's Books*. (London: Gower Publishing Company, 1982), 135.

10. Zena Sutherland, Dianne L. Monson, and May Hill Arbuthnot, *Children and Books*, 6th ed. (Glenview, Ill.: Scott, Foresman, 1981), 50.

11. Anne Pellowski, "Internationalism in Children's Literature" in *Children and Books*, ed. Zena Sutherland et al., 598–99.

12. Donna E. Norton, *Through the Eyes of a Child* (Columbus, Ohio: Charles E. Merrill, 1983), 93–94, 488–512.

13. "Ten Quick Ways to Analyze Children's Books for Sexism and Racism," in *Guidelines for Selecting Bias-Free Textbooks and Storybooks* (New York: Council on Interracial Books for Children, n.d.), 24–26.

14. Beilke to public librarians and school library supervisors in the fifty largest cities of the United States, 3 January 1984.

15. Susan F. Tait, 14 March 1984, Seattle, Washington; Toni Bernardi, 31 January 1984, Portland, Oregon; Patricia J. Sullivan, 6 March 1984, San Francisco,

California; Linda F. Crismond, 25 January 1984, Downey, California; Joe Sabatini, 1 March 1984, Albuquerque, New Mexico; and Margaret Trivison, 28 February 1984, San Diego, California to Beilke.

16. Venora W. McKinney, 3 February 1984, Milwaukee, Wisconsin; Amanda S. Rudd, 19 January 1984, Chicago, Illinois; Celeste Chin, 30 January 1984, Detroit, Michigan; Ann Strachan, 16 January 1984, Indianapolis, Indiana; Jacob S. Epstein, 12 January 1984, Cincinnati, Ohio; W. H. Garnar, 13 January 1984, Louisville, Kentucky; and Nan Sturdivant, 24 January 1984, Tulsa, Oklahoma, to Beilke.

17. Christine Behrmann, 18 June 1984, New York, New York; Linda Perkins, 24 January 1984, Buffalo, New York; Maria Teresa Braga, 1 February 1984, Newark, New Jersey; Kit Breckenridge and Geoffrey Wilson, 31 January 1984, Philadelphia, Pennsylvania; Hardy R. Franklin, 22 February 1984, Washington, D.C.; Casper L. Jordan, 13 January 1984, Atlanta, Georgia; and Anne S. Boegen, 11 January 1984, Miami, Florida, to Beilke.

18. Unknown, 17 January 1984, Seattle, Washington; Christine W. Poole, 20 January 1984, Portland, Oregon; Janet K. Minami, 16 February 1984, Los Angeles, California; Elinor McCloskey, 7 February 1984, Albuquerque, New Mexico; Diane A. Ball, 2 February 1984, Dayton, Ohio; Kathryn Miller, 21 February 1984, Indianapolis, Indiana; Christina Woll, 17 January 1984, El Paso, Texas; and Carol A. Kearney, 23 January 1984, Buffalo, New York, to Beilke.

19. Eileen Tway, ed., *Reading Ladders for Human Relations*, 6th ed. Urbana, Ill.: National Council of Teachers of English, 1983.

Chapter 6.
Change, Guidelines, and Selected Resource Centers

1. Margaret R. Marshall, *Libraries and Literature for Teenagers* (London: André Deutsch, 1975), 166–86.

2. Leona Daniels, "The 34th Man: How Well Is Jewish Minority Culture Represented in Children's Fiction?" in *Issues in Children's Book Selection: A School Library Journal / Library Journal Anthology* (New York: R. R. Bowker Company, 1973), 95.

3. Nathan A. Josel, "Public Library Material Selection in a Bilingual Community," *Catholic Library World* 54 (October 1982): 113.

4. Ibid., 114.

5. Ibid., 115.

6. Ibid.

7. "Proyecto LEER—Its Mission and Services," Proyecto LEER *Bulletin* 16 (Fall 1980): 1.

8. Marie Zielinska to Beilke, 3 March 1983, "Multilingual Biblioservice Book Selection Guidelines," revised 1 January 1983 (Ottawa, Ontario, Canada: National Library of Canada, 1983), 1–2, in English and French.

9. "Vietnam: A Teacher's Guide," *Focus on Asian Studies*, special issue 1 (Fall 1983): 28.

10. Wendell Wray, "Criteria for the Evaluation of Ethnic Materials," in *Ethnic Collections in Libraries*, ed. E. J. Josey and Marva L. DeLoach (New York: Neal Schuman Publishers, 1983), 24–35.

11. Joshua A. Fishman, *Language Loyalty in the United States* (The Hague, The Netherlands: Mouton, 1966): 22–23.

12. Phyllis J. Kimura Hayashibara, "A Guide to Bilingual Instructional Materials for Speakers of Asian and Pacific Island Languages," AMERASIA *Journal* 5 (1978): 110.

13. Christina Bratt Paulston, "Bilingualism and Education," in *Language in the USA*, ed. Charles A. Ferguson and Shirley Brice Heath (New York: Cambridge University Press, 1981), 482.

14. "Title VII Network Centers and Fellowship Programs," supplement to FORUM (January 1982), 1–3.

15. Abdel-Messih Daoud and Marianne Celce-Murcia, "Selecting and Evaluating a Textbook," in *Teaching English as a Second or Foreign Language*, ed. Marianne Celce-Muria and Lois McIntosh (Rowley, Mass.: Newbury House Publishers, 1979), 302.

16. Ibid., 302–3.

17. E. Jeanne López-Valadez, ed., *Curriculum Materials for Bilingual and Multicultural Education: An Annotated Bibliography*. Volume I: Spanish Language Arts (Arlington Heights, Ill.: Bilingual Education Service Center, 1976).

18. Marcia Seidletz, ed., *Curriculum Materials for Bilingual and Multicultural Education: An Annotated Bibliography*. Volume II: Content Area Materials — Spanish and English (Arlington Heights, Ill.: Bilingual Education Service Center, 1979).

19. Maria Medina Swanson, Introduction, to López Valadez, *Curriculum Materials* I: iii.

20. López-Valadez, *Curriculum Materials* I: 58.

21. Seidletz, *Curriculum Materials* II: 77.

22. Ibid., 81–82.

23. Rudolph C. Troike, "Research Evidence for the Effectiveness of Bilingual Education," Report from the Center for Applied Linguistics and National Clearinghouse for Bilingual Education (Rosslyn, Va.: National Clearinghouse for Bilingual Education, 1978).

24. Muriel Saville-Troike, *Bilingual Children: A Resource Document*, Bilingual Education Series 2 (Arlington, Va.: The Center for Applied Linguistics, 1973), 47–49.

25. Iris C. Rotberg, "Federal Policy in Bilingual Education," *American Education* 18 (October 1982): 33; originally in *Harvard Educational Review* 52 (May 1982).

26. Richard Rodriguez, "A Minority Scholar Speaks Out," *American Education* 18 (November 1982): 2–3.

27. Peggy Rubens, *Vocational Education for Immigrant and Minority Youth*, Information Series 257 (Columbus, Ohio: The National Center for Research in Vocational Education, 1983), 27–28.

28. Ibid., 13.

29. Ibid.

30. Ibid.

31. Ibid., 25.

32. Ibid., 25–26.

33. Ibid., 29–30.

34. National Institute of Education, EPIE *Career Education* S*E*T (New York: EPIE Institute, n.d., v.

35. Ibid., 22–54.

36. Ibid., 85–94.

37. Thomas A. Andersen, ed., *Guide to Implementing Multicultural Non-sexist Curriculum Programs in Iowa Schools* (Des Moines, Iowa: State of Iowa, Department of Public Instruction, 1976), 17–18.

38. Marcia D. Olson, ed., *Arts Education in Iowa Schools: Multicultural Nonsexist Education*. (Des Moines, Iowa: State of Iowa, Department of Public Instruction, 1980, 8–15.

39. Guy Bensusan, "Art," in Foster, *Sourcebook of Hispanic Culture*, 112–30.

40. Ibid., 117.

41. Ibid., 116.

42. Catharine E. Wall, "Art," in Foster, *Sourcebook of Hispanic Culture*, 187–200.

43. Robert C. Small, Jr., "Meeting Bias in Children's and Adults' Literature," *Phi Delta Kappan* 63 (May 1981): 664.

44. Oscar Uribe, Jr., Tamara Altman, and James Vasquez, "A Mexican American Perspective," in *Perspectives on School Print Materials: Ethnic, Non-Sexist and Others*, A Handbook Developed by STRIDE—A General Assistance Center Project; Coordinator Wayne E. Rosenoff (San Francisco, Calif.: Far West Laboratory for Educational Research and Development, 1975), 19–20.

45. Ibid., 26.

46. Helen W. Painter, "Translations of Traditional and Modern Material," in *Evaluating Books for Children and Young People*, ed. Helen Huus (Newark, Del.: International Reading Association, 1968), 43.

47. Shirley Sun, Tamara Altman, and James Vasquez, "A Chinese-American Perspective," in *Perspectives on School Print Materials*, 43–55.

48. Ibid., 46.

49. Small, "Meeting Bias," 664.

50. Ibid., 665.

51. "School Books Get Poor Marks: An Analysis of Children's Materials about Central America," *Interracial Books for Children Bulletin* 13, nos. 2 and 3 (1982): 3–12.

52. State Department of Public Instruction, *Textbook Criteria and Basic Principles* (Dover, Del.: State Department of Public Instruction, 1973), 13.

53. Ibid., 14–18.

54. Office of Equal Educational Opportunities to Assist DESE Staff to Implement DESE Policies, *Guidelines for Materials and Presentations* (Pierre: South Dakota Division of Elementary and Secondary Education, 1978), 52–53.

55. Ibid., 61–64.

56. Frank Chin, "Where I'm Coming From," *Interracial Books for Children Bulletin* 7, nos. 2 and 3 (1976): 24–25.

57. *Selection of Instructional Materials* (Baltimore: Maryland State Department of Education, Division of Library Development and Services, School Media Services Office, 1981), 6–7.

58. Ibid., 6–8.

59. Irving M. Levine, "Bolstering the Family through Informal Support Groups: A Group Identity Approach," An address by the Director, Institute on Pluralism and Group Identity, American Jewish Committee, presented at the conference "The American Family 1978: Human Values and Public Policy," cosponsored by the Philadelphia chapter of the American Jewish Committee and St. Joseph's College, Philadelphia, Pennsylvania, 30 April 1978, 9–10. Reprints available from Institute on Pluralism and Groups Identity, 612 West 57th Street, New York, N.Y.

60. *Vegetable Soup: Parent-Teacher Guide* (Albany: The University of the State of New York, State Education Department, Bureau of Mass Communications, n.d.), 16.

61. Marguerite Baechtold and Eleanor Ruth McKinney, *Library Service for Families* (Hamden, Conn.: The Shoe String Press, 1983), 182–83, 97–100, 106–8, 189–222.

62. Frances Smardo and Velma Schmidt, "Using Books to Help Teachers and Children Develop Multicultural Awareness," *The Southeastern Librarian* 34 (Summer 1984): 47.

63. Melinda Greenblatt, "Expanding Children's Programming in School and Public Libraries," *Wilson Library Bulletin* 54 (October 1979): 99–102.

64. Geraldine L. Wilson, "The Values Conveyed in Children's Toys," *Interracial Books for Children Bulletin* 12, no. 6 (1981): 3–9.

65. Harry W. Sartain, "Research Summary: Family Contributions to Reading Attainment," in *Mobilizing Family Forces for Worldwide Reading Success*, Selected Papers, Part 3, Seventh IRA World Congress on Reading, Hamburg, August 1–3, 1978 (Newark, Del.: International Reading Association, 1981), 13.

66. Henry G. Burger, "Adapting Education Cross-Culturally," in *Cultural Challenges to Education: The Influence of Cultural Factors in School Learning*, ed. Cole S. Brembeck and Walker H. Hill (Lexington, Mass.: Lexington Books, D.C. Heath and Company, 1973), 116–17.

67. Ibid., 117.

68. Ibid.

69. "Sources of Children's Books from Other Countries and in Other Languages," a mimeographed list (New York: Information Center on Children's Cultures, 1982), 1.

70. Lucretia M. Harrison, "Acquiring Foreign Children's Books," *School Library Journal* 25 (December 1978): 25.

71. Marie Zielinska and Irena Bell, "Selection and Acquisition of Library Materials in Languages Other than English: Some Guidelines for Public Libraries," in *Collection Building*, vol. 2 (New York: Neal Schuman Publishers, 1980), 7–28.

72. National Education Association, *Selected and Annotated Bibliography on Teaching Refugee Children: Indochinese, Haitian, Cuban* (Washington, D.C.: National Education Association, 1980).

73. Nathan A. Josel, interview with Beilke, Washington, D.C., 8 January 1985.

74. Theodore Andersson, *A Guide to Family Reading in Two Languages: The Preschool Years* (Rosslyn, Va.: National Clearinghouse for Bilingual Education, 1981 (ERIC Document Reproduction Service ED 215 560), 63–65.

75. Max Rosenberg, "Criteria for Evaluating the Treatment of Minority Groups and Women in Textbooks and Other Learning Materials," in Banks, *Teaching Strategies*, 2d 461–64.

76. Ibid., 463.

77. Ibid., 465–72.

78. Martha E. Dawson and Geneva Gay, eds., *Guidelines for Avoiding Biases in Instructional Television*, prepared for the production of the Essential Learning Skills Television Project series THINKABOUT (Bloomington: Indiana Agency for Instructional Television, 1978), 1–15.

79. Marie-Noëlle Icardo, "Immigrés et bibliothèques aux Etats-Unis," *Bulletin des bibliothèques de France* 27 (1982): 195–202.

LIST OF
BACKGROUND READINGS

Acuña, Rodolfo. *Occupied America: The Chicano's Struggle toward Liberation.* San Francisco: Canfield Press, 1972.

_____. *The Story of the Mexican-Americans.* New York: Litton Educational Publishing, 1967.

Allman, T. D. "Cambodia: Nightmare Journey to a Doubtful Dawn." *Asia Magazine* 4 (April 1982): 8–15.

Anaya, Rudolfo A. *Bless Me Ultima.* Berkeley, Calif. Tonatiah International, 1972.

Babín, María Teresa and Stan Steiner, eds. *Borinquen: An Anthology of Puerto Rican Literature.* New York: Knopf, 1974, o.p.

Baker, Houston A., Jr. *Three American Literatures: Essays in Chicano, Native American and Asian American Literature.* Introduction by Walter J. Ong. New York: Modern Language Association of America, 1982.

Boswell, Thomas D., and James R. Curtis. *The Cuban-American Experience: Culture, Images, and Perspectives.* Totowa, N.J.: Rowman and Allanheld, 1984.

Buaken, Manuel. *I Have Lived with the American People.* Caldwell, Idaho: Caxton Printers, 1948.

Bulosan, Carlos, Jr. *America Is in the Heart: A Personal History.* Seattle: University of Washington Press, 1973. Reprint of 1946 edition.

Buttinger, Joseph. *The Dragon Defiant: A Short History of Vietnam.* New York: Praeger, 1972.

Canillo, Alex, et al., eds. *Pinoy: Know Yourself: An Introduction to the Filipino American Experience.* Santa Cruz: Third World Teaching Resource, University of California, 1975.

Carrion, Arturo Morales, ed. *Puerto Rico: A Political and Cultural History*. New York: W. W. Norton, 1983.

Casal, Lourdes. "A Bibliography of Cuban Creative Literature: 1958–1971." *Cuban Studies Newsletter* 2 (June 1972) 2–29.

———. "The Cuban Novel, 1959–1969, An Annotated Bibliography." *Abraxas* 1 (Fall 1970): 77–92.

Chandler, David P. *A History of Cambodia*. Boulder, Colo.: Westview Press, 1983.

Chen, Jack. *The Chinese of America*. New York: Harper & Row, 1982.

Chin, Frank, Jeffrey Paul Chan, Lawson Fussao Inada, and Shawn Hsu Wong, eds. *Aiiieeeee! An Anthology of Asian-American Writers*. New York: Doubleday, 1975. o.p.

Coedès, G. *The Making of Southeast Asia*. Trans. by H. M. Wright. Berkeley: University of California Press, 1983.

Cordasco, Francesco, and Eugene Bucchioni, eds. *The Puerto Rican Community and Its Children on the Mainland: A Source Book for Teachers, Social Workers and Other Professionals*. 3d rev. ed. Metuchen, N.J.: Scarecrow Press, 1982.

———. *The Puerto Rican Experience: A Sociological Sourcebook*. Totowa, N.J.: Littlefield, 1975. Reprint of 1973 edition.

A Core Collection of Print Material for Libraries Serving the Spanish Speaking of the Southwest. Compiled by the Arizona Chapter of REFORMA. Tucson: University of Arizona Libraries, 1978.

DeLeon, Arnoldo. *They Called Them Greasers: Anglo Attitudes toward Mexicans in Texas, 1821–1900*. Austin: University of Texas Press, 1983.

Department of the Army. *Area Handbook for Laos*. Washington, D.C.: U.S. Government Printing Office, 1972.

Dicker, Laverne Mau. *The Chinese in San Francisco: A Pictorial History*. Preface by Thomas W. Chinn. New York: Dover Publications, 1980.

Fagen, Richard R., Richard A. Brody, and Thomas J. O'Leary. *Cubans in Exile: Disaffection and the Revolution*. Stanford, Calif.: Stanford University Press, 1968.

Fitzpatrick, Joseph J. *Puerto Rican Americans: The Meaning of Migration to the Mainland*. Englewood Cliffs, N.J.: Prentice-Hall, 1971.

Foster, David William, ed. *Sourcebook of Hispanic Culture in the United States*. Chicago: American Library Association, 1982.

Fox, Geoffrey E. *Working-Class Emigrés from Cuba*. Palo Alto, Calif. R & E Research Associates, 1979.

Garrett, Wilbur E. "No Place to Run: The Hmong of Laos." *National Geographic* 145: (January 1974): 78–111.

———. "The Temples of Angkor: Will They Survive?" *National Geographic* 161 (May 1982): 548–51.

Glick, Clarence E. *Sojourners and Settlers: Chinese Migrants in Hawaii*. Honolulu: University Press of Hawaii, 1980.

Golding, Morton J. *A Short History of Puerto Rico.* New York: New American Library, 1973. o.p.

Gomez, David. *Somos Chicanos: Strangers in Our Own Land.* Boston: Beacon Press, 1973.

Grebler, Leo, Joan W. Moore, and Ralph C. Guzman. *The Mexican-American People: The Nation's Second Largest Minority.* New York: Free Press, 1970.

Hall, D. C. *A History of South-East Asia.* 4th ed. New York: St. Martin's, 1981.

Hauberg, Clifford A. *Puerto Rico and Puerto Ricans.* New York: Hippocrene Books, 1974. o.p.

Hawkins, John N. *Teacher's Resource Handbook for Latin American Studies: An Annotated Bibliography of Curriculum Materials Preschool through Grade Twelve.* Vol. 6, UCLA Latin American Center Reference Series, published with the assistance of the Curriculum Inquiry Center at UCLA. Los Angeles: UCLA Latin American Center Publications, 1975.

Hernandez Miyares, Julio E. "The Cuban Short Story in Exile: A selected Bibliography." *Hispania* 54 (May 1971): 384–85.

Herrera, Diane, ed. *Puerto Ricans and Other Minority Groups in the Continental United States: An Annotated Bibliography.* New foreword and supplemental bibliography by Francesco Cordasco, Detroit: Blaine, Ethridge, Books, 1979.

Hsu, Francis L. K. *The Challenge of the American Dream: The Chinese in the United States.* Belmont, Calif.: Wadsworth, 1971.

Huerta, Jorge A. *Chicano Theater: Themes and Forms.* Binghamton, N.Y.: Bilingual Review Press, 1982.

Jacobs, Paul, Saul Landau, and Eve Pell. *To Serve the Devil: A Documentary Analysis of America's Racial History and Why It Has Been Kept Hidden.* 2 vols. New York: Random House, 1971.

Keller, Gary D., and Francisco Jimenez, eds. *Hispanics in the United States: An Anthology of Creative Literature.* Ypsilanti, Mich.: Bilingual Press, 1980. (Department of Foreign Languages and Bilingual Studies, 106 Ford Hall, Eastern Michigan University, Ypsilanti, Mich. 48197.)

Kim, Elaine H. *Asian American Literature: An Introduction to the Writings and Their Social Context.* Philadelphia: Temple University Press, 1982.

Kim, Hyung-chan, and Cynthia C. Mejia. *The Filipinos in America, 1898–1974.* Dobbs Ferry, N.Y.: Oceana Publications, 1976.

Kim, Hyung-Chan, and Wayne Patterson, eds. and comp. *The Koreans in America, 1882-1974. A Chronology and Fact Book.* Dobbs Ferry, N.Y.: Oceana Publications, 1974.

Kim, Illsoo. *New Urban Immigrants: The Korean Community in New York.* Princeton: Princeton University Press, 1981.

Kim, Warren Y. *Koreans in America.* Reedley, Calif.: Po Chin Chai Printing Co. Ltd., 1971. (Available in the United States from Rizzoli International

Publications, Foreign Language Department, 712 Fifth Avenue, New York, N.Y. 10022.)

Kitano, Harry H. L. *Japanese Americans: The Evolution of a Subculture.* 2d ed. Englewood Cliffs, N.J.: Prentice-Hall, 1976.

Koh, Kwang Lim, and Hesung C. Koh, eds. *Koreans and Korean Americans in the United States. Their Problems and Perspectives. A Summary of Three Conference Proceedings, 1971–1973.* New Haven, Conn.: East Rock Press, 1974.

Kung, Shien-woo. *Chinese in American Life: Some Aspects of Their History, Status, Problems and Contributions.* Seattle: University of Washington Press, 1962. o.p.

Lasker, Bruno. *Filipino Immigration to Continental United States and Hawaii.* Salem, N.H.: Ayer Co., 1969. Reprint of 1931 edition.

Lazo, Mario. *Dagger in the Heart: American Policy Failures in Cuba.* New York: Guild Books, 1970, o.p.

Lebar, Frank, and Adrienne Suddar. *Laos: Its People, Its Society, Its Culture.* New Haven: Human Relations Area File Press, 1960.

Lee, Rose Hum. *The Chinese in the United States.* Hong Kong: Hong Kong University Press, 1960. o.p.

Levine, Barry B. *Benjy Lopez: A Picaresque Tale of Emigration and Return.* New York: Basic Books, 1980.

Lewis, Gordon K. *Puerto Rico: Freedom and Power in the Caribbean.* New York: Monthly Review Press, 1975. Reprint of 1963 ed.

Lipp, Solomon. "The Anti-Castro Novel." *Hispania* 58 (May 1975): 284–96.

Lopez, Adalbert, and James Petras, eds. *Puerto Rico and Puerto Ricans: Studies in History and Society.* New York: Halsted Press, 1974.

Lutheran Immigration Services. *The Hmong: Their History and Culture.* New York: Lutheran Immigration Services, 360 Park Ave., New York, N.Y. 10010, n.d.

Lyman, Stanford M. *The Asian in the West.* Reno, Nev.: Desert Research Institute, University of Nevada System, 1970.

————. *Chinese Americans.* New York: Random House, 1974.

McWilliams, Carey. *North from Mexico: The Spanish-Speaking People of the United States.* New York: Greenwood Press, 1968. Reissue of 1949 edition.

Martin, Patricia Preciado. *Images and Conversations: Mexican Americans Recall a Southwestern Past.* Tucson: University of Arizona Press, 1983.

Meier, Matt S., and Feliciano Rivera. *The Chicanos: A History of Mexican-Americans.* New York: Hill & Wang, 1972.

Meining, D. W. *Southwest. Three People in Geographical Change, 1600–1970.* New York: Oxford University Press, 1971.

Menton, Seymour, *Prose Fiction of the Cuban Revolution.* Austin: Institute for Latin American Studies, University of Texas, 1975.

Mesa-Lago, Camelo, ed. *Cuban Studies / estudios cubanos.* Pittsburgh, Penn.: Center for Latin American Studies, University Center for International Studies, University of Pittsburgh, 1970–. Semiannual.

Mohr, Eugene V. *The Nuyorican Experience: Literature of the Puerto Rican Minority*. Westport, Conn.: Greenwood Press, 1982.

Moore, Joan W., with Alfredo Cuellar. *Mexican Americans*. Englewood Cliffs, N.J.: Prentice-Hall, 1976.

Moquin, Wayne, with Charles Van Doren eds. *A Documentary History of the Mexican-Americans*. New York: Praeger, 1971.

Morales, Royal F. *Makibaka: The Filipino American Struggle*. Los Angeles: Mountainview Publishers, 1974.

Munoz, Alfredo N. *The Filipinos in America*. Los Angeles: Mountainview Publishers, 1971.

Nakanishi, Don T., and Marsha Hirano-Nakanishi, eds. *The Education of Asian and Pacific Americans: Historical Perspectives and Prescriptions for the Future*. Phoenix, Ariz.: Oryx Press, 1983.

Natella, Arthur A., Jr., comp. and ed. *The Spanish in America, 1513-1979*: A Chronology and Fact Book. rev. ed. Dobbs Ferry, N.Y.: Oceana Publications, 1980.

Nguyên, Du. *The Tale of Kiêu: A Bilingual Edition of Truyên Kiêu*. Translated and annotated by Huỳnh Sanh Thông, with a historical essay by Alexander B. Woodside. New Haven: Yale University Press, 1983.

Ortego, Philip D., ed. *We are Chicanos. An Anthology of Mexican-American Literature*. New York: Washington Square Press, 1973.

Osborne, Milton, *Southeast Asia: An Introductory History*. Rev. ed. Boston: Allen & Unwin, 1982.

Outsama, Kao, *Laotian Themes*. New York: Regional Bilingual Training Resource Center, Board of Education, June 1977.

Padilla, Elena. *Up from Puerto Rico*. New York: Columbia University Press, 1958.

Perazic, Elizabeth. "Little Laos, Next Door to Red China." *National Geographic* 117 (January 1960): 46–69.

Petersen, William. *Japanese Americans: Oppression and Success*. New York: Random House, 1971. o.p.

Prohlas, Rafael J., and Lourdes Casal, eds. *The Cuban Minority in the U.S.: Preliminary Report on Need Identification and Program Evaluation. Final Report for Fiscal Year 1973*. 2d ed. rev. Washington, D.C.: Cuban National Planning Council, 1974.

Quan, Robert Seto, with Julian B. Roebuck. *Lotus among the Magnolias: The Mississippi Chinese*. Foreword by Stanford M. Lyman. Jackson: University Press of Mississippi, 1982.

Quinsaat, Jesse, ed. *Letters in Exile: An Introductory Reader on the History of Filipinos in America*. Los Angeles: UCLA Asian American Studies Center, University of California, 1976.

Quintana, Helena, with the assistance of Richard Allen Moore, IV. *A Current Bibliography on Chicanos 1960–1973, Selected and Annotated. No. 3, Sources*. Albuquerque: The University of New Mexico, UNM Bookstore, 1974.

Rivera, Edward. *Family Installments: Memories of Growing Up Hispanic*. New York: Penguin Books, 1983.

Robles, Al, et al., eds. *Liwang: Literary and Graphic Expressions*. San Francisco: Liwang Publications, 1975.

Romano-V., Octavio I. "The Anthropology and Sociology of the Mexican-Americans." *El Grito* 2 (Fall 1968): 13–26.

———. "The Historical and Intellectual Presence of Mexican-Americans." *El Grito* 2 (Winter 1969): 32–47

Romo, Ricardo. *East Los Angeles: History of a Barrio*. Austin: University of Texas Press, 1983.

Rosaldo, Renato, Robert A. Calvert, and Gustav L. Seligmann, eds. *Chicano: The Evolution of a People*. Minneapolis, Minn.: Winston Press, 1973.

Schon, Isabel. *A Bicultural Heritage: Themes for the Exploration of Mexican and Mexican-American Culture in Books for Children and Adolescents*. Metuchen, N.J.: Scarecrow Press, 1978.

———. *A Hispanic Heritage: A Guide to Juvenile Books about Hispanic People and Cultures*. Series 2. Metuchen, N.J.: Scarecrow Press, 1985.

Silen, Juan Angel. *We, The Puerto Rican People: A Story of Oppression and Resistance*. Translated from Spanish by Cedric Belfrage. New York: Monthly Review, 1971.

Sommers, Joseph, and Tomas Ybarra-Frausto. *Modern Chicano Writers: A Collection of Critical Essays*. Englewood Cliffs, N.J.: Prentice-Hall, 1979.

Steiner, Stan. *Fusang, The Chinese Who Built America*. New York: Harper & Row, 1979.

———. *La Raza: The Mexican-Americans*. New York: Harper & Row, 1969.

Stoddard, Ellwyn R. *Mexican-Americans*. New York: Random House, 1973.

Sue, Stanley, and Harry H. L. Kitano, eds. "Asian Americans: A Success Story?" *Journal of Social Issues* 29 (1973): 1–209.

Sung, Betty L. *The Story of the Chinese in America*. New York: Macmillan, 1972. o.p.

Sunoo, Brenda Paik, ed. *Korean American Writings: Selected Material from INSIGHT, Korean American Bimonthly*. New York: Insight, 1975.

Tachiki, Amy, Eddie Wong, and Franklin Odo, eds. *Roots: An Asian American Reader*. Los Angeles: Continental Graphics, 1971. o.p.

Tambiah, S. J. *Buddhism and the Spirit Cults in Northeast Thailand*. Cambridge, Eng., Cambridge University Press, 1970.

Tebell, John, and Ramon E. Ruiz. *South by Southwest: The Mexican-American and His Heritage*. New York: Doubleday, 1969.

Thernstrom, Stephan, Ann Orlav, and Oscar Handlin, eds. *Harvard Encyclopedia of American Ethnic Groups*. Cambridge, Mass.: Harvard University Press, 1980.

Thomas, Hugh. *Cuba — The Pursuit of Freedom*. New York: Harper & Row, 1969.

Trejo, Arnulfo D. *Bibliografia Chicana: A Guide to Information Sources.* Vol. 1 in the Ethnic Studies Information Guide Series. Detroit, Mich.: Gale Research Company, 1975.

————, ed. *The Chicanos: As We See Ourselves.* Tucson: University of Arizona Press, 1979.

Vek, Huong Tiang. *Ordeal in Cambodia: One Family's Escape from the Khmer Rouge.* San Bernadino, Calif.: Here's Life Publishers, 1980.

"Vietnam: A Teacher's Guide." *Focus on Asian Studies.* Special Issue 1 (Fall 1983): 1–27.

Vuong G. Thuy. *Getting to Know the Vietnamese and Their Culture.* New York: Frederick Ungar, 1976.

Wagenheim, Kal. *Puerto Rico: A Profile.* rev. ed. New York: Praeger, 1976. o.p.

————, ed. *The Puerto Ricans: A Documentary History.* New York: Doubleday, 1973. o.p.

Weber, David J., ed. *Foreigners in Their Native Land: Historical Roots of the Mexican Americans.* Albuquerque: University of New Mexico Press, 1973.

White, Peter T. "Kampuchea Awakens from a Nightmare." *National Geographic* 161 (May 1982): 590–623.

Whitmore, John K., ed. *An Introduction to Indo-Chinese History, Culture, Language and Life.* Ann Arbor: Center for South and Southeast Asian Studies, University of Michigan, 1979.

Wilson, Robert A., and Bill Hosokawa. *East to America: A History of the Japanese in the United States.* New York: William Morrow, 1982.

Wu, Cheng-Tsu, ed. *"Chink!": A Documentary History of Anti-Chinese Prejudice in America.* New York: World Publishing Company, 1972.

Wu, William F. *The Yellow Peril: Chinese Americans in American Fiction, 1850–1940.* Hamden, Conn.: Archon Books-The Shoe String Press, 1982.

Wyndham, Robert. *Chinese Mother Goose Rhymes.* New York: Putnam, 1982.

INDEX